Mar 2016

Folktales from the Arabian Peninsula

WORLD FOLKLORE SERIES ADVISORY BOARD

FOLKTALES FROM THE ARABIAN PENINSULA

TALES OF BAHRAIN, KUWAIT, OMAN, QATAR, SAUDI ARABIA, THE UNITED ARAB EMIRATES, AND YEMEN

NADIA JAMEEL TAIBAH AND MARGARET READ MACDONALD

World Folklore Series

LIBRARIES
UNLIMITED™
An Imprint of ABC-CLIO, LLC
Santa Barbara, California • Denver, Colorado

Library of Congress Cataloging-in-Publication Data

Taibah, Nadia Jameel.
   Folktales from the Arabian Peninsula : tales of Bahrain, Kuwait, Oman, Qatar, Saudi Arabia, the United Arab Emirates, and Yemen / Nadia Jameel Taibah and Margaret Read MacDonald.
      pages cm. — (World folklore series)
   Includes bibliographical references and index.
   ISBN 978-1-59158-529-9 (pbk : alk. paper) — ISBN 978-1-4408-4207-8 (ebook)
1. Tales—Arabian Peninsula.   2. Folk literature, Arabic—Arabian Peninsula.   I. MacDonald, Margaret Read, 1940-   II. Title.
   GR275.T35   2016
   398.20953—dc23   2015013879

ISBN: 978-1-59158-529-9
EISBN: 978-1-4408-4207-8

19 18 17 16 15   1 2 3 4 5

This book is also available on the World Wide Web as an eBook.
Visit www.abc-clio.com for details.

Libraries Unlimited
An Imprint of ABC-CLIO, LLC

ABC-CLIO, LLC
130 Cremona Drive, P.O. Box 1911
Santa Barbara, California 93116-1911

This book is printed on acid-free paper ∞

Manufactured in the United States of America

CONTENTS

FOLKTALES FROM SAUDI ARABIA
Tales shared by Nadia Jameel Taibah

SAUDI ARABIA: OTHER TALES
Retold by Margaret Read MacDonald

FOLKTALES FROM BAHRAIN

FOLKTALES FROM KUWAIT

FOLKTALES FROM OMAN

FOLKTALES FROM QATAR

FOLKTALES FROM THE UNITED ARAB EMIRATES

FOLKTALES FROM YEMEN

ARABIC PROVERBS AND PROVERB TALES

INTRODUCTION

The marvelous legendry of the Arab peoples from ancient times is well known through *The Thousand and One Nights*, often called *The Arabian Nights*. You will find many editions of those stories in your library. The stories in these collections vary, and only some of them are from the Arabian Peninsula. A collection featuring other tales of marvels, some with earlier origins even than *The Thousand and One Nights*, can be found in the excellent *Fabled Cities, Princes & Jinn from Arab Myths and Legends* by Khairat Al-Saleh (New York: Schocken, 1985).

In *Tales from the Arabian Peninsula*, we offer simpler stories, those told today by the people who live in the countries of the Arabian Peninsula. We have limited ourselves to only tales from the Arabian Peninsula itself and do not include tales from the other Arabic-speaking countries.

THE ARABIAN PENINSULA

Travel and Trade

The Arabian Peninsula's position has placed it at the crossroads of travel and trade throughout time. Archeological digs all along the Arabian Gulf Coast have revealed remains of the towns of ancient peoples, such as the Dilmun civilization, a Bronze Age trading center from around 3,000 BC. The Dilmun civilization was centered in present-day Bahrain and also had a town on Failaka Island in present-day Kuwait. Their Bahrain city was a two-day sail from Mesopotamia and a stop for ships to restock supplies and water before heading across the Indian Ocean to India. It was also a trading center for pearls, copper, and other goods and a center of ship building.

Some of the oldest evidence of inhabitants on the Arabian Peninsula are the 40,000-year-old Stone Age sites found in Yemen, at the southwestern end of the peninsula. This area also claims various biblical and Koranic sites. It is believed to be the land of the Queen of Sheba, and some believe that Shem, the son of Noah, settled there and founded the Semite people. On the Red Sea side of the peninsula, trade routes were also busy. Frankincense and myrrh as well as pearls were traded. The Saba people who ruled around 1000 BC had quite an advanced civilization. They built houses that were several stories high and constructed a dam that was 2,000 feet wide (609 meters) for irrigation.

On the southeastern end of the peninsula, in Oman, a 200 BC fortress, perhaps much older, has been found inland, just at the edge of Rub al-Khali (the Empty Quarter desert) at Shisr. Stone

Age sites have also been found near there. From Salalah, a semitropical seaside city with date palms, small frankincense trees, and enough rainfall for some crops, the road climbs an escarpment to reach a flat, rocky plain. Over 170 km inland across this plain one reaches Shisr. Here archeological digs have revealed evidence of an ancient trade route. Frankincense traveled this route across the Rub al-Khali (the Empty Quarter desert). The large port city of Sumhuram has also been excavated in present-day Salalah.

Oman became a major trading center, sending out sailing dhows to the island of Zanzibar and other East African ports. Following the trade winds, they were able to reach India, and from there they could continue on a very long voyage all the way to China. Frankincense and myrrh were a major part of their trade, and for a time, slaves and ivory were brought from Zanzibar, which served as a slave depot for the East African interior.

The Omanis were remarkably skilled navigators, and it is suggested that the story of Sinbad the Sailor, a popular tale found in *The Thousand and One Nights*, holds many factual accounts of an Omani voyage. An Omani navigator accompanied the Portuguese explorer Vasco da Gamma and showed him how to reach India—a great voyage of exploration for a European, but a regular route for the Omani sailors. The sailors could navigate with nothing more than a piece of cardboard and a string, with which they could estimate their position by their relationship to specific stars.

Frankincense

Frankincense, which thrives in the Al-Mahrah and Hadramat regions of Yemen and in the Dhofar region of southern Oman, has been prized over the centuries as an incense to burn in religious rituals. The Greek scholar Herodotus mentions that over two and a half tons of Frankincense were burned in the Babylonian temple of Baal. The Roman emperor Nero had an entire year's worth of frankincense from the Arabian Peninsula burnt as a tribute at the funeral of his wife. Egyptians used frankincense in embalming. And the Bible tells us that three wise men brought gifts of frankincense, myrrh, and gold to the baby Jesus.

Camels

Camel caravans became possible after a special saddle was invented around 1,200 BC. This allowed camel caravans to travel across the vast stretches of desert that cover the interior of the Arabian Peninsula. Now frankincense, myrrh, and other goods could pass by land, rather than having to be transported by ship.

The camel proved an unusually reliable means of transport because it can live on almost any plants or grasses it encounters. And humans can then live on the camel's milk or slaughter an occasional camel for meat. The Omani tribal leader Mahbrook Massan, who recounted our stories of "Abu Nawas, the Trickster" and "A Djinn Story," told us that when he was a child, his family wandered for weeks at a time away from the water of their home oasis at Shisr. While living in the rocky desert, his mother fed them by milking the camels. This provided both nourishment and liquid. The camels' bodies also provided warmth and shelter when the night temperatures became frigid, and they provided shade in the heat of the day.

Introduction

Pilgrimages

After the rise of Islam, sites in Saudi Arabia became important pilgrimage destinations. Each Muslim is expected to visit Mecca at least once in his or her life, unless financial constraints or health make this impossible. And Medina, the second holiest city in Saudi Arabia, is often visited as well. This travel put Saudi Arabia at the heart of considerable travel from all parts of the Islamic world. Today, over 3 million pilgrims reach Mecca each year during the Hajj (pilgrimage) season, the beginning of the 12th month of the Islamic calendar. And more pilgrims, perhaps as many as 4 million, visit Mecca and Medina throughout the year to perform *Omraa* (Umrah), which is a visit to the Ka'ba performed at a time other than the Hajj season.

Invasions

At times, various peoples, including the Assyrians, Babylonians, Greeks, Persians, Ottoman Turks, and Portuguese, invaded the Arabian Peninsula. Each group ruled for a time and then was overthrown. Today, the countries of the Arabian Peninsula are all independent and ruled by leaders of the specific Arabic tribes who have controlled these areas since the 1800s or earlier.

Oil Wealth

The discovery of oil changed everything for this area. With money came the possibility to build schools, hospitals, and roads. The royal families who controlled the countries amassed enormous wealth. And because the royal families in many countries are so extensive, this wealth was spread through many households. Most of the countries also chose to distribute some of the oil wealth among their citizens. This was done with direct monetary gifts, stock in the oil enterprises, or land grants. Most of the countries charge no taxes on their people, and health care and education are usually free. In some cases, utilities such as water and electricity are also provided at no charge.

Because citizenship carries perks with it, strict requirements have been established for claiming citizenship. Adherence to Islam is usually one. The residence of your family in the area since before the advent of the oil boom is another. It is difficult or impossible for new arrivals to claim citizenship. Thousands of workers must be brought in from other countries to maintain the workforce needed in these growing economies. So the number of noncitizens residing in some Arabian Peninsula countries far exceeds the number of citizens.

Using the oil monies, the cities in this region are growing at a furious pace. Shallow seas are being filled in to create even more land for building, and entire islands, such as the Palm Jumeirah (shaped like the branches of a palm) and the World Islands (shaped like countries of the world) in Dubai and the Pearl (a ring of reclaimed land with high-rise apartments and shops) in Doha, the capital of Qatar, have been created and filled with high-end developments. Dubai boasts the tallest building in the world, the Burj Khalifa.

The countries honor the arts with museums, such as the stunning Museum of Islamic Art in Doha, and performance venues, such as the Muscat Royal Opera House in Oman. Each country sponsors a historical museum, such as the handsome Bahrain National Museum. The Al Tayebat International City Museum in Jeddah has 300 rooms centered around a 300-year-old palace. And archeological sites such as the Al Balid Archeological Park in Salalah are found in many locations. There are dynamic events such as the Sharjah International Book Fair. Doha is also home to one of the world's foremost television networks, Al Jazeera.

Islam

The people of the Arabian Peninsula are of the Muslim faith. Prophet Mohammad was born in Mecca around AD 570. The Ka'ba had been a pilgrimage site for centuries at the time Prophet Mohammad was born, but it contained images of various gods. Prophet Mohammad insisted on reverence to only one true god. The word "Allah" means "God" in Arabic. Today, all Muslims turn toward Mecca to pray, and all pray to Allah.

There are Five Pillars (rules) of Islam:

Stating with conviction, "There is no God but God and Prophet Mohammad is his messenger."
Praying five times daily (dawn, noon, midafternoon, sunset, evening).
Giving charity (a portion of wealth given to those less fortunate)
Fasting during the month of Ramadan.
Performing the Hajj, the pilgrimage to Mecca.

OLD AND NEW, SIDE BY SIDE

Oil money is bringing rapid change to the Arabian Peninsula. A new chapter in the region's history is being written.

The modern towers above the old souk shops in Kuwait City.

The new springs up behind the old in Kuwait City.

THE COUNTRIES OF THE ARABIAN PENINSULA

Bahrain

The Al-Khalifa family left Kuwait after the Al-Sabah family took control in 1756. The Al-Khalifa moved to the Bahrain area and became the rulers of this region.

Bahrain is an island country only 257 square miles in total land mass (665 sq km). Bahrain Island is connected by causeways to Muharraq Island and Sitrah Island. A few other small islands, including the Hawar Islands, are considered a part of Bahrain's territory. Bahrain lies just 15 miles off the coast of Saudi Arabia. The King Fahd Causeway, constructed by the Saudi government, was completed in 1986, connecting Bahrain to the mainland. A causeway is also planned between Qatar and Bahrain.

In Bahrain, 2.8 percent of the land is usable for growing crops, and 92 percent is desert. About 5 percent of Bahraini ground is covered with over 350,000 tombs left by the ancient Dilmun people. Fields of lumpy tomb mounds can be seen in many places, and archeological concerns limit the usage of these lands.

Of the Bahraini population, 62.4 percent are Bahraini Arab. The rest of the population includes Asians, other Arabs, Iranians, and some Europeans, Americans, and Australians in specialized jobs.

Kuwait

At the top of the Arabian Peninsula, on the Arabian Gulf, sits Kuwait, a country not quite as big as New Jersey. Kuwait shares a sometimes-disputed border with Saudi Arabia. The two countries have decided to share the oil-rich land of this border region. North of Kuwait lies Iraq, which tried to annex Kuwait in 1990, resulting in the Gulf War. After the Gulf War, the United Nations established the current border. Several islands in the Arabian Gulf are claimed by Kuwait, including Warbah, Failaka, and the large Bubiyan Island, which is connected to the mainland by a bridge.

Most of Kuwait is flat, sandy, or gravelly desert, though a few ridges of low hills do lie in the desert, as well as sand dunes. Freshwater is now provided by desalinization plants. Less than 1 percent of Kuwait is farmland, growing olives, dates, and fruits. But irrigation enables crops such as tomatoes and cucumbers now.

Fish traps.

Fishing boats in Fahaheel harbor, Kuwait.

Kuwait has a long coastline, so fishing is an important industry. At one time, pearl fishing was a busy occupation, but the use of cultured pearls today has destroyed that industry. Though the pearl fishing industry is gone, the sea still is an important source of income for Kuwaitis, both for fishing and for trade.

People

Most of Kuwait's population is concentrated near the coastal cities of Kuwait City (with nearby Al-Ahmadi and Al-Jahra) and Al-Fuhayhil, and less than 50 percent of the residents are Kuwaiti citizens. Many residents are *bidouns* (different from Bedouins). These are Arab people who do not have citizenship in Kuwait and do not have citizenship in any other country either. And there are thousands of temporary service providers living in Kuwait: construction and household workers from Asia; teachers and technicians from the United States, Great Britain, and Australia; and many others.

Because of oil revenues that go into the government treasury and into the personal bank accounts of members of the ruling Al-Sabah family, many Kuwaiti citizens are required to work only a few hours per day or not at all. Revenues from the oil wells are used by the government to subsidize food purchases and to provide free housing. Education and health care are free, and there are no taxes. Original citizens must have been residing in Kuwait prior to 1920 and must be Muslim and speak Arabic. The Al-Sabah family has ruled Kuwait since 1756 and has a large extended family, so many Kuwaitis have royal family connections that allow them to share in the oil wealth.

TENTING

Kuwaitis love to remember their past as a desert people. So each year, when the weather is agreeable, they set up family tents out on the desert sands. Often many families group their tents together. Electric lights are put up, and gas tanks are brought in for cooking. Satellite dishes provide TV and Internet access. Though these families often have large, comfortable homes or even mansions to live in, they love this annual camping experience. They drive out in their pickup trucks or SUVs for a weekend or for several weeks.

A Kuwaiti tent. Photo by Margie Deemer.

Black tent, March 2013. Note satellite dishes beside tent.
Photo by Margie Deemer.

Tenting in Kuwait, January 2012. Notice the tall klieg lights and the many gas
tanks. This is set up for long term comfort.

Oman

Oman is the third-largest country on the Arabian Peninsula, a little larger than Colorado. It occupies the southwestern portion of the Arabian Peninsula, plus a strategic small holding adjacent to
the United Arab Emirates, which could control access through the Strait of Hormuz between the
Arabian Peninsula and Iran. All shipping between the Arabian Gulf and the Gulf of Oman, leading
to the Indian Ocean, passes through this 39-mile-wide gap.

The northern part of Oman has rocky, hilly terrain and includes the large cosmopolitan city of
Muscat. The southernmost portion of Oman receives more rainfall than most of the Arabian Peninsula, as monsoons from the Indian Ocean drop some rainfall there. So there is a coastal region of
date palms, frankincense trees, and some crop-growing possibilities.

Oman's extensive coastline includes several useful harbors; shipbuilding and oceangoing
trading expeditions were important in the country's history. Inland, the terrain rises in an escarpment to a dry plateau of gravel, which reaches into the sandy Rub al-Khali (Empty Quarter).

From 1698 to 1896, Oman governed the East African island of Zanzibar, off the coast of Tanzania. Descendants of Zanzibaris brought to Oman as slaves still live in Oman. Because of the trade routes, peoples from Baluchistan, across the sea in Iran, and from India have also settled in Oman at various times. The percentage of foreign workers in Oman is not as overwhelming as in some of the other Arabian Peninsula countries: over 70 percent of the population of Oman are Omani citizens.

In 1970, Sultan Qaboos bin Said al Said became ruler of Oman. He defeated a communist insurgency attacking from Yemen and then began to modernize his country, building roads, schools, hospitals, and universities. As a patron of the arts, he created a highly respected symphonic orchestra composed of young Omanis trained in classical music.

Saudi Arabia

Saudi Arabia covers about 80 percent of the Arabian Peninsula. Most of the country lies in the massive Arabian desert, which is semidesert and scrubland. In the south of the peninsula lies the 888,730-square-mile (2,250,000 sq km) Rub al-Khali (Empty Quarter), an enormous sand desert. In the southwestern province of Asir is the 10,279-feet-high (3,133 m) Mount Sawda.

Wikipedia lists the 2013 population of Saudi Arabia as 26.9 million. The *CIA World Factbook* states that 21 percent of the population is foreign nationals. The country is trying to limit this workforce to 20 percent through a program of training and incentives for Saudi citizens.

Saudi Arabia is ruled by the house of Saud, descendants of Ibn Saud, who consolidated the tribes of Saudi Arabia into one country in 1932. King Abdullah reigned after 2005, when his half brother King Faud died. In 2015 King Abdullah passed away at the age of 90 and was succeeded by his 79 year old half brother Salman bin Abdulaziz Al Saud.

Nadia Jameel Taibah, who lives in Jeddah, describes her country:

> The Kingdom of Saudi Arabia enjoys a long and rich history that traces its roots back to the earliest civilizations of the Arabian Peninsula. The region's ancient nomadic peoples developed a deep love for the land as well as a strong sense of independence. With the advent of Islam in the seventh century, tribes and clans were unified under one religion, which is Islam.
>
> The Kingdom of Saudi Arabia comprises almost four-fifths of the Arabian Peninsula, an area about one-third the size of the continental United States. The eastern part of Saudi Arabia is a plateau that begins with the great Nafud desert in the north, continues along the Arabian Gulf, and culminates in the south in the world's largest sand desert, the Rub Al-Khali (Empty Quarter). To the west of this plateau is the Najd, the heartland of the peninsula, known for its spectacular escarpments and gravel and sand deserts. The capital city of Riyadh is located in the Najd. A chain of mountains in western Saudi Arabia runs parallel to the Red Sea. The Hijaz region along the Red Sea contains the holy cities of Makkah [Mecca] and Madinah [Medina].
>
> The Ka'ba is the House of Allah located in the city of Mecca. Muslims visit the Ka'ba at least once in their lifetime, and this visit is the holy event known as Hajj. Hajj is performed during a special period of the year.

The Ka'ba was built before Prophet Mohammad's or Prophet Isa's lifetime. It was built by Prophet Ibrahim and his son Ismael. They were among the first people to visit that part of the world. Allah commanded Ibrahim and Ismael to build the Ka'ba so that people could come from far and wide in order to worship Allah.

The Ka'ba was built from stone and clay. People used to go inside the Ka'ba and pray. When the population grew, people prayed on the outside in the direction of the Ka'ba. The holy ground surrounding the Ka'ba is called Haram.

The new building of Haram can hold two million people with three stories. It is all air-conditioned and covered with white marble. Plenty of Persian rugs are covering the floor, and the high ceiling is covered with beautiful writing of the name of Allah, Prophet Mohammad, and some Koranic verses. The Ka'ba is covered with black dress that is especially made and changed every year at Hajj time. The upper part is hemstitched with gold in Koranic verses.

In the city of Madinah is a Haram for "Prophet Mohammad's Mosque." It was built by Prophet Mohammad and his Companions when he immigrated from Makkah to Madinah. He was buried, along with the two of the best companions, Abu Bakr Alsadeek and Omar Ibn Alkattab, at this mosque.

United Arab Emirates

In 1971, the rulers of Abu Dhabi, Dubai, Sharjah, Ajman, Umm al-Quwain, and al-Fujairah formed a federation, the United Arab Emirates. In 1972, Ras al-Khaimah joined.

The United Arab Emirates population is only 19 percent Emirati. Another 23 percent of the residents are other Arabic-speaking peoples, or from Iran. Asians make up 50 percent of the population, as workers from India, Pakistan, Indonesia, and the Philippines come as construction workers and household servants and to fill other low-paying jobs. The remaining 8 percent of the population are highly paid Westerners and other foreigners who fill jobs as technicians and teachers and provide other skilled services.

Abu Dhabi

Abu Dhabi is the largest of the emirates, around 375 square miles, approximately 87 percent of the United Arab Emirates land.

The Al-Nahyan family rules Abu Dhabi today. They descend from the Bani Yas Bedouin, some of whom migrated to the island of Abu Dhabi in 1793 because of the fresh water there. The family originally came from the Liwa Oasis area in the south of the country, near the Rub al-Khali desert, which covers much of the Arabian Peninsula.

Abu Dhabi has a long coastline along the Arabian Gulf. The coastal features include salt flats and mangrove groves. The city of Abu Dhabi itself sits on and around an island connected to the mainland by bridges.

Dubai

Dubai is ruled by the Al Maktoum family. Their clan, the Al Bu Falasah, broke away from the Abu Dhabi Bani Yas group in 1833 and founded Dubai. Located on the Arabian Gulf, Dubai has white sands that support some grasses and date palms, areas with large dunes, some salt flats, and in the west, the Western Hajar Mountains, with their gorges and waterholes. Dubai also controls a small enclave, Hatta, adjacent to Oman.

Ras al-Khaimah

Ras al-Khaimah consists of a portion of land located on the Arabian Gulf west of Umm al-Quwain and a smaller portion surrounded by Sharja's holdings and Al Fujayrah. It is ruled by a member of the Al-Qasimi clan. The Qawasim were great seafarers and controlled the Straits of Hormuz at one time.

Sharjah

The city of Sharjah sits on the Arabian Gulf, but Sharjah also owns the small Gulf of Oman enclaves of Kalba, Dibba Al-Hsin, and Khor Fakkan and a third small enclave, Nahwa, adjacent to Oman. The city of Sharjah has grown to the point where it connects with Dubai and Ajman, forming one huge metropolitan area. Sharjah is controlled by the Al-Qasimi family.

Al-Fujairah

The al-Fujairah emirate is controlled by the Al Sharqi family. Al-Fujairah is located on the Gulf of Oman, with two portions separated by a bit of Sharjah land and a third portion adjacent to Oman. This emirate is almost totally mountainous and receives enough rainfall for farmers to produce an annual crop.

Umm al-Quwain

The Al Mu'alla lineage of the Al Ali tribe rule in Umm al-Quwain. With only 292 square miles (755 km), Umm al-Quwain is the second-smallest of the emirates. Umm al-Quwain has a coastline with sandy islets, mangrove swamps, and creeks.

Ajman

The Al Nuaimi are the ruling tribe of the emirate of Ajman. The tiny country also controls Masfut, a small agricultural exclave. Ninety-five percent of the residents of Ajman live in Ajman City. Dubai, Sharjah, and Ajman together form a large metropolitan area.

Qatar

Qatar occupies a peninsula jutting into the Arabian Gulf. It is about the size of Connecticut. The only country it has borders with is Saudi Arabia. Bahrain lies only 24.8 miles (40 km) across the sea to the north, and a causeway is planned. Only about one-fifth of the population of Qatar is actually Qatari. The rest are foreign workers: about 20 percent are Arabs from other countries, 18 percent are Pakistani, 18 percent are from India, and 10 percent are Iranian. The rest include skilled workers from Europe, the United States, Australia, and other countries. In 2012, 94 percent of the workforce in Qatar was foreign.

Wealth from oil reserves enables the Qatari citizens to live well. In 2012, Qatar was the richest country in the world, based on per capita income. Fourteen percent of households were considered millionaires. Qatari citizens might receive various perks, such as free education, free land to build homes on, government jobs, and no taxes. Many receive monies from oil investments. Members of the royal family, and this includes thousands of individuals, receive a share of the oil revenues.

Only 2 percent of Qatar is capable of growing crops, and desalinization plants are necessary to fill the needs of the area for freshwater. Oasis wells, which once could provide adequate water, cannot begin to provide enough water for the growing population, and overpumping can drain the aquifers that supply them. The peninsula is sand or gravel desert, mostly flat, with some sand dunes, and with low limestone outcroppings in the west.

The Al Thani family of the Banu Tamin tribe have ruled Qatar since 1825.

Yemen

Located at the southeastern tip of the Arabian Peninsula, Yemen holds a strategic place on the Gulf of Aden and the narrow entrance to the Red Sea, the Bab el Mandeb Strait. Yemen is the second-largest country on the Arabian Peninsula, about the size of Colorado and Wyoming combined. The coastal regions of southern Yemen receive enough rainfall to produce crops, especially the Hadramat region. The interior is desert and merges into the Rub al-Khali. Some of the tallest mountains on the peninsula are located in Yemen, with the Jabal an Nabi Shu-ayb the highest, at 12,336 feet (3,760 m).

Frankincense and myrrh grow well in the Hadramat and other areas of Yemen, and this area, along with Oman, was once a center of incense trade. The Old Testament tells of the Queen of Sheba visiting King Solomon in Palestine and bringing frankincense and myrrh. The country of Sheba was Saba, which included present-day Yemen and parts of Saudi Arabia.

Yemen has had a troubled past. North Yemen and South Yemen have disagreements, and the government has changed several times in recent years.

LUQMAN THE WISE

Let's begin our exploration of Arabic folktales with these tales of a pan-Arabic wise man.

Many stories are told about the wise man Luqman. It is said that one day while Luqman was napping under a tree, an angel came to him in a dream. The angel said that Allah would give him a gift. He could choose either to be a king or to be wise. Without hesitating, Luqman chose wisdom. When he awoke, Luqman realized that he felt in harmony with nature and now understood many things. He thanked Allah for this wondrous gift.

Later Luqman was captured by slavers and sold as a slave. He remained calm and accepted his slavery, so his owner respected him. One day, his owner decided to test him. He asked Luqman to kill a sheep and bring him the most valuable parts of the sheep. Luqman prepared the tongue and heart and brought them to his owner. Later, the man asked Luqman to slaughter a sheep and bring him the worst parts. Luqman brought the tongue and heart. When questioned about this, Luqman explained that when good, the tongue and heart are the best possible things. But when bad, they are the worst. It is true that a man with a good heart speaks kindness with his tongue and calms things, while a man with a bad heart speaks evil and creates dissension.

Later, Luqman became highly regarded for his wisdom. Many of the fables we know today as Aesop's Fables are also attributed to Luqman.

Luqman was also known for his wise sayings. He is quoted as saying, "Talk in a low voice. If loud voices could get things done, asses would be building houses every day." "When people see a rich man eating a snake, they say it is for medicinal reasons. When they see a poor man eating a snake, they say he is hungry." "Don't repeat everything you hear, and don't talk about everything you see." Many of Luqman's sayings are popular today, such as, "A bird in the hand is better than a thousand flying about the sky."

A Muslim Hadith tells that Luqman was once asked how he came to his high position. "By speaking truthfully, being faithful to trust put in me, and leaving alone things that do not concern me."

In one tale, Luqman asks God for long life. God agrees to let him chose a lifespan of seven generations of an animal of his choice. He chooses the lifespan of a falcon. He then adopted a baby falcon and raised it as his companion. The falcon lived for 80 years. But one day it died. Now Luqman journeyed to the mountains, found another falcon nest, and retrieved another baby falcon. And so it went until the seventh falcon was his companion. He called this seventh falcon, Lubud, which means "time." Lubud lived on the top of a jebel (peak), and Luqman lived at the bottom. After 80 years, when he awoke one morning and made his way to the top of the jebel, he found that Lubud was very weak. "Lubud do not die! If you die you take my life with you!" But Lubud closed his eyes and passed on. So lying down, Luqman also closed his eyes and passed.

Luqman apparently maintained his strengths well into his later years though. His servant girl was once asked how his eyesight was holding up. "Not very well," she replied. "Yesterday he was watching a couple of ants cross the ceiling and he could hardly make out which trail was that of the male and which that of the female."

FOLKTALES FROM SAUDI ARABIA

Tales shared by Nadia Jameel Taibah

ANIMAL TALES

THE DOVE, THE PARTRIDGE, AND THE CROW

A long, long, long time ago, there was a Bedouin tribe named Benazin. They were looking for a new land because they had used all their land's water and plants. So they decided to scour the area of the countryside around them.

They released three different kinds of birds: the crow, the dove, and the partridge. They trusted the crow very much because the crow proved to be a very hard worker and he had good vision. They trusted the dove and the partridge too because they could both fly for a long distance without getting tired.

So the three birds flew off at the same time. After a short period of time, the crow arrived at a very green land with plenty of water. He stopped there. And that was in the south direction.

He stopped there and thought to himself, "Bah Bah Bah! I can go back to them and tell them I couldn't find anything. I would have the whole land to myself. I would have the food, and I'll have the plants and the water to myself. I will be the king. It will all belong to me. Nobody is going to share the food with me. Nobody is going to boss me around. I will be the king, and this is my kingdom." He liked his idea very much.

With the sad news, and sadness on his face, he returned to the tribe. "As far as I traveled, there is nothing but desert and desert and desert. Not even a small stalk or a blade for the cattle to feed on. Don't go there! Especially to this direction." Pointing to the south, of course.

"Don't go to the south! Trust me. There is nothing over there. More desert . . . and you will get lost. Trust me. Trust me."

Well, the tribe was very sad. But they decided to wait for the other two birds to arrive.

Finally, the other two birds arrived, with happy news and happy faces. They came from the same direction. They came from the south.

They said with one voice, "Ann . . . ann . . . ann . . . ann. Plenty of water! So soft the grasses there that even a newborn child could rest on them."

"Go! Go to this direction. Go to the south! It is so good over there. It is so green. And plenty of water."

Now the tribe was very confused. The crow said, "Don't go to the south." And the other two birds said, "Go to the south." So they decided to have a vote. And finally they voted to follow the dove and the partridge direction to the place they had described.

When they arrived to that green land, surprisingly they discovered that the crow was a liar. So after they settled down in their new land, they took the crow to justice. Because of his lie, they painted the crow black all over. And so he remains to this day.

The dove and partridge they rewarded. They stained the feet of one with festive red henna and lined the eye of the other one with black kohl. Up to this day, you can see that the dove walks on pink feet, and the partridge has beautiful black-ringed eyes.

THE FOX, THE WOLF, AND THE LION

One day, a lion, a wolf, and a fox made a pledge. They decided that whatever game they caught they would share. First off, they came across a rat hole. The lion pushed a stick inside it and shook it around. The rat in the hole thought the stick was a snake, and it ran out of the hole. The fox jumped and caught the rat easily.

They went on, looking for something else to catch. There was a rabbit! The three animals surrounded it, and the lion killed it with one swat of his right hand. Now they had two things to divide.

Next the three saw a gazelle hiding in some bushes. The three took chase and eventually caught up with it and killed it. They looked at their hunt and decided it was enough and wanted to divide it.

The lion looked at the wolf and asked, "How do you think we should divide our prey?"

The wolf said, "You get the gazelle, I get the rabbit, and fox gets the rat."

The lion roared angrily, and with one swat of his right hand, he killed the wolf.

Then the lion turned to the fox. "And how do YOU think we should divide our prey?"

The fox thought quickly and replied, "The gazelle for your lunch, the rabbit for your dinner, and the rat is a snack for you in between meals."

The lion, admiringly, looked at the fox and asked, "Who taught you how to make such fair division?"

Bowing and backing away, the fox muttered, "I learned it from the wolf."

THE ANT AND THE LOUSE

Here is a cumulative tale that would sound more poetic in Arabic. It has a rather dour ending, but the rhythm of the original would make it fun.

The ant and the louse
went up the sand dune.
They found a little grain.
They cooked it in a pot.
The louse wanted to taste it,
But the ant hit the louse with the cooking spoon.
The louse cried, "Oh people of the continent! Because I was mistreated,
Ride on your denying donkey. It denies the bush."
The people said, "What defeats you, bush?"
The bush said, "I am the bush; sheep eat me."

"What defeats you, sheep?"
"I am sheep; knife kills me."
"What defeats you, knife?"
"I am knife; the fire heats me."
"What defeats you, fire?"
"I am fire; rain extinguishes me."
"What defeats you, rain?"
"I am rain; I raise grass."
"What defeats you, grass?"
"I am grass; horse eats me."
"What defeats you, horse?"
"I am horse; the boy rides on me."
"What defeats you, boy?"
"I am boy; death takes me."
"What defeats you, death?"
"I am death; I take you, hug you, and throw you into your mother's tummy (earth)."

RIDDLE STORIES

SIGNS

A sultan was once approached by a mysterious-acting wise man. This wise man entered the sultan's court, knelt before the sultan, and proceeded to make strange signs with his hands. No one could understand what he meant by these signs.

All of the wisest men in the court were called in to observe the stranger's gesticulations. But no one could understand what he meant.

The sultan's vizier was concerned. "Our kingdom's reputation depends on this one mysterious wise man. All the scholars and all the philosophers that have raised our academic reputation have failed to translate one man's riddles."

The sultan agreed with this assessment of the situation. But he put the problem back in the hands of the vizier.

"You must search our kingdom for someone who will save us from our precarious situation. Someone who can answer this wise man's enigmatic signs. And if you do not do it, I swear by the creator of my crowned head, I will have your turbaned one."

The vizier rushed out of the palace, desperate to find someone to take the challenge. In the marketplace, he came upon a strange sight. An old man was sitting, surrounded by a crowd, eating hard-boiled eggs, one after the other. There was a whole pile of eggs beside him, and he just kept swallowing without pause. When only one egg was left, he put it in his pocket and started to leave the marketplace. This man's actions seemed as strange as those of the wise man at the palace. So the vizier decided to bring *him* to the palace.

The old man was alarmed when he saw all of the courtiers and soldiers and the sultan himself.

"This is the man who can solve our predicament?" asked the sultan.

"Well, show him the riddle," the sultan commanded the visiting wise man.

The visitor smiled and nodded. He held out his pointer finger in an upward position. The old man immediately raised his pointer and second finger.

Then the guest raised his arm toward the ceiling, and his opponent raised his and then swept it down with the other arm. The guest smiled.

The visitor took out a box and opened it. The old man glanced inside it and saw a small yellow chick and instantly drew out the egg that was in his pocket.

After this interlude, the wise guest was quite satisfied, for his whole face lit up, happy that someone had understood his meaning.

"At last you have brought forth a man wise enough to match my challenge," he said. "Congratulations on the wisdom of your kingdom."

When the old man was taken of the court, the sultan requested that his guest explain.

"Oh, my dear sultan, when I raised my pointer, I of course meant to say, 'Praised is Allah, the one and only.' And his reply was to raise his pointer and index, meaning to say, 'The one who has no partner.' By lifting my arm, I meant, 'Praised is he who had raised the sky without columns.' And he brought his arm down, meaning, 'And praised is he who has lain the earth over water.' I took out my chick to say, 'Praised is he who has brought the living out of the dead.' And he took out the egg, my lord, to say, 'And praised is he who has brought the dead out of the living!'"

And so saying, the visiting wise man left the court and returned to his own country.

The sultan laughed so hard at the simplicity of it all, and the court joined him in his relief.

"Strange how this simple old man outwitted my cultured scholars! Bring him so I can reward him, for he shall be greatly honored."

Of course, the poor old man was dismayed to be dragged before the sultan yet again. "What now, my lord? What more do you want from me?"

"I want to ask you, old man, how you understood my guest's strange signs?"

"Oh, you mean that crazy man at your court? He put up one finger to show that he could tear out my old tired eye with his finger! So I put up two fingers to reply that I could tear out both of his with mine! And then he gestured that he could hang me from the ceiling, so I told him that I could toss him down onto the floor! Then, to add more to his malice, he took out his chick to bait me with it, so I told him, 'So what? I have an egg!'"

The sultan roared with laughter. Sometimes the very meek are just what is needed to preserve the kingdom's reputation.

JOUHA STORIES

JOUHA AND HIS DONKEYS

Once Jouha was driving ten donkeys loaded with goods to the city. He loaded up ten donkeys, put them in a line, and counted them out. One, two, three, four, five, six, seven, eight, nine, ten.

Then Jouha got onto one of the donkeys and set off for town. But after a while, it occurred to him that he had better look behind and count to make sure all the donkeys were still in line. To his horror he could only see NINE donkeys behind him!

He got off and checked each donkey carefully. But now there were indeed ten donkeys. Relieved, he got back on his donkey and continued on his way.

After he had ridden for a way, he realized he should check again to make sure all the donkeys were still following. But, "Oh no!" One was missing again!

He jumped down and ran back to line them up and check to see which was missing. But there were ten there after all. Such a problem!

After repeating this several times, it finally dawned on Jouha that every time he RODE on a donkey, one of the others would slip off. So he sighed and got down from his donkey.

"I will just have to walk," he decided. "It is better to walk on foot and gain one donkey than to mount and lose one of them."

So he walked all the way to town.

HUMOROUS TALES

THE POOR LADY'S PLAN

A long, long time ago, there was an old poor lady who lived in a very poor hut. The only thing she had was an old rug covering the floor of her hut. She had a very wealthy neighbor, the head judge of Mecca town. This poor lady used to go every day to the farmers' market to trade her own products for food. She had an old sack that she used to carry on her back so she could carry the vegetables from the market. One day, this poor lady came from the market, and she found out that her only rug was not on the floor.

She said to herself, "I am sure I didn't move it. Or maybe I sold it and I forgot."

While she was looking around for the rug, she noticed that the rug was rolled up in one of the dark corners of her poor hut. Well, she was surprised. She was sure that she had not cleaned her house for a long time. And all of the sudden she noticed big filthy shoes coming out of the rug.

"My dear Allah," she thought, "here is a burglar, and I am an old lady, ALL ALONE BY MYSELF. Now if I tried to run away, he would definitely catch me. If I screamed, nobody is going to hear me before he comes out and kills me."

The old poor lady kept thinking and thinking. She was so terrified.

Finally, she arrived at this brilliant idea: "Mmmm . . . I will bring my drums and start singing with a loud voice, like I am having a party." So she started singing with the old sack filled with vegetables on her back.

> Ajoza fi dahraha bostan ya rabee kelkata alrahman.
> Ajoza fi dahraha bostan ya rabee kelkata alrahman.
> Ajoza fi dahraha bostan ya rabee kelkata alrahman.
> (Which means, an old lady with garden on her back, and that is Allah's creation.)

At that moment, the servant of the judge's family was depluming and cleaning a goose for lunch by the kitchen window. She heard the voice of the old poor lady.

"Since I started working at the judge's family, I have not been able to have any fun," the servant thought. "It has been a long time since I attended any parties, singing or dancing. I am just going to join the old lady and have some fun." She left everything, the goose, the cooking, and she went to sing and dance.

> Kunt Bantuf Alweza we jet Anhazalli Hazza.
> Kunt Bantuf Alweza we jet Anhazalli Hazza.
> Kunt Bantuf Alweza we jet Anhazalli Hazza.
> (Which means, I was depluming the goose, and I came to dance.)

The singing became a little louder.

The judge's wife was just finishing her cup of coffee, and she needed more. So she called the servant to bring her more coffee.

"Hey, servant, servant, servant!" With a loud voice she shouted, but nobody answered.

On her way to the kitchen, looking for the servant, she heard singing voices coming from the old lady's hut. She looked from the window and saw the two ladies. The servant and her neighbor were singing and dancing. The wife felt very sorry about herself.

"Since I got married to this judge, I have not been able to attend any weddings or parties," the wife thought. "I need to go with them to sing and dance. Let us have some fun! Who needs to eat or drink?"

> *Sebt Alqahwa wa Alfinjan We Jeet Arqos Fi Almeedan.*
> *Sebt Alqahwa wa Alfinjan We Jeet Arqos Fi Almeedan.*
> *Sebt Alqahwa wa Alfinjan We Jeet Arqos Fi Almeedan.*
> (Which means, I left the coffee and the cup and came to dance in the field.)

The singing became much louder.

It was time for the judge to come home for lunch. He knocked at the door, calling for his wife or the servant. But nobody was there.

"That is strange," the judge said. "Where is everybody? Hey, lady! Hey, servant!"

Nobody answered, so he went to the kitchen, following the loud singing voice. He saw from the kitchen window his wife, the servant, and the old lady singing and dancing.

"Since I became the judge of Mecca, I have not been able to have some time off to myself," the judge grunted. "I really forgot how people sing or dance. I am just going to go and have some fun, singing and dancing with my wife. Losing respect for a while is not really a big deal."

So he went wearing his own *kaffieh* (head cloth), singing with his hoarse voice:

> *Ana Alqadi Bi emmati Wa Jeet Arqos Maa' meerati.*
> *Ana Alqadi Bi emmati Wa Jeet Arqos Maa' meerati.*
> *Ana Alqadi Bi emmati Wa Jeet Arqos Maa' meerati.*
> (Which means, I am the judge with my *kaffieh* who came to dance with my wife.)

The burglar heard the voice and the identity of the last singer. He got frightened, rolled himself out of the rug, and tried to run as quickly as possible.

But the old lady started screaming, "A burglar, a burglar!"

The judge was faster. He caught the burglar and put him into jail! The old lady's plan worked very well.

MAGICAL STORIES

THROW YOUR PUMPKIN AND PICK ME UP

There was once a house where a woman and her loving daughters lived. And those daughters would beg their mother every time she prepared to leave for the marketplace to get them a pumpkin, for their hungry mouths were watering for some pumpkin stew. But the woman would forget each time she went, and they would be sorely disappointed. The one time she remembered, however, was on a hot sunny day.

The marketplace was busy and colorful, with all sorts of foodstuffs. When finally her arms were loaded with household groceries, she spotted, from faraway, a man selling one large plump-looking pumpkin, just the thing she needed to treat her girls with. After she approached and paid for it, she discovered how heavy it was. Pull and drag as she might, that pumpkin was the heaviest thing she'd ever carried. She eventually lifted it along with her groceries, but it was the hardest feat.

On her way home, she was stopped on the dirt path by an old dark-skinned man who clutched her robes as if he would never let go.

"Throw your pumpkin and lift me up, mother," he said.

"What? What madness is this? You want me to carry *you* when I could hardly lift the pumpkin?" she demanded.

"God be kind to you. Please throw your pumpkin and pick me up!" he begged again, while the astounded woman continued to refuse.

The pedestrians on the narrow street all gathered around and took pity on the old man.

"Can't you find it in your heart to give him his wish?" they said to her.

When she found that she was compelled to please the old man, she did indeed lift him up onto her back, and God knows how she managed to carry pumpkin, vegetables, old man, and all. The trip took twice as long as it should have taken, and she only got home to her worried daughters, who were sitting anxiously by the lookout window to watch for her arrival, when the muezzin called for late noon prayers.

On her doorstep, she dropped the old man with a great groan, for her poor back was thoroughly abused.

"Here, now, I've reached my doorstep. Please leave to your own business, old man."

"No. You must open your door and take me inside."

"What catastrophe is this?" the woman asked, more to herself than to anyone else. "Pray that Allah rid you of the devil and leave me be."

But he proved to be quite obstinate. He shook his dark, ancient head and refused to budge from her doorstep and refused to let her leave him unless she let him inside.

She wanted dearly to scream, but she shut her lips firmly and opened her door for the old man to hobble in.

"Climb the stairs and carry me with you."

The poor woman was ready to faint by now. But she decided that he must want something, and she wanted to find out what it was.

On the top landing, she saw her girls standing in a row. They all inquired, in a baffled state, about the old stranger who was comfortably astride their mother's back. Their mother explained to them her wretched story with the old man and how he came to be there. She wasted no time telling them that it was all because of that wretched pumpkin.

When she was finished, she dropped him on the floor. Before they all went into their living quarters, they turned to him and said, "All right, uncle, you must leave now."

"No. You must cook the pumpkin and feed me."

"So that is why you clung to our mother! You're hungry and want to eat!" they cried. "Stay at the door, and we'll bring you some of it."

The stew was stewed to perfection, and its warm, homey odor filled their home. They poured some of it in a bowl for the weak old man.

"You have no excuse to stay here now, old man," they said to him when the eating was done. "Please leave our house."

"Never. You must make a bed for me and put me to sleep," he replied.

"What's that you say? The last thing we need is a strange man when we're lone women in a house at night!" cried the mother.

As much as she pleaded and begged with him, he would not depart. Therefore, the mattress was spread.

"He might be very tired, the poor man. We'll let him sleep here just the one night," the girls said to their mother, coaxingly.

"Get a blanket and cover me," he croaked when they thought he would finally drift to sleep and leave them be.

"Why would you need a blanket? The nights are hot nowadays," the woman muttered.

The blanket was brought to him, however. Covered from head to toe with the dingy blanket, the rigid lumpy form spoke in a muffled voice, "You must bring a cane and beat me."

And that, they were only too happy to do! The long rods of wood crashed down on him with such ferocity, but never a word he said. In fact, they continued to wallop his bony frame until man and floor were one.

They didn't realize it until a few seconds had passed. They were hitting nothing now. The man had disappeared right beneath their eyes. The mother knelt gingerly to uncover the spot of floor that they were hitting. In the place where the old man would have been lying, there was a pile of sparkling golden coins.

"It is gold!" said one of the girls.

"It's a miracle!" cried the other.

It was with thankful eyes and sudden understanding that the woman and her daughters gathered their newly found treasure.

The little family was quite happy with their gold, for such an amount of it they rarely encountered. They thought eagerly that it would be grand if they could weigh it and see how much it was worth. Therefore, the youngest daughter was sent to their neighbor to borrow a set of copper scales they knew she had.

Now, this particular neighbor happened to be very beady-eyed and very inquisitive about other people's affairs. Her eyes nearly popped out when she was told by the young girl that her mother wanted to weigh something, and her feet bounced on their balls. She wanted desperately to know what her neighbor could be weighing. So she stuck a pitted date that was kneaded into sticky dough on one of the scales and gave the set to the little girl with a generous smile.

When the set was sent back to her, she wasted no time in peeking to see if any proof had stuck to the dough she'd hidden. And sure enough, there was a single golden coin glimmering forlornly back at her. How came her poor neighbor with such riches?

She could not bear it anymore. She set out grimly and pounded on her neighbor's shabby door. When the usual formalities were over and done with, her feverish question sailed out of her mouth before she could control herself.

"How did you ever manage to get your hands on that gold? One of your coins was stuck to my copper set." She handed the coin to her. "All of us are poor in this neighborhood. Do tell me!"

"I shall tell you. It's a very strange story . . ."

The curious woman listened to her intently, and after that, a steady plan had formed in her mind. When the sun arose upon the next day, she was already up and ready. She shook her lazy daughters awake from their slumber.

"Mother, why are you waking us at such an early hour?" they asked crankily.

"I'm going to the marketplace, and you must ask me to get you a pumpkin," she said shortly and matter-of-factly.

"But you know we don't like pumpkin and can't stand to put it into our mouths!" they protested.

"Nevertheless, you must ask me for it!"

She repeated herself several times before she got what she wanted, for the girls were very reluctant.

"All right! Get us a pumpkin . . . but we won't eat it!"

And their mother was quite satisfied with this reply. She set off, with determination quite apparent on her face, to the marketplace where she might find one large orange pumpkin similar to that of her neighbor. Her desire was immediately spotted, for her eyes were keen and searching like those of a hawk's. She bought it, feeling no regret at losing precious money over something her family would not eat. It would soon be repaid and more.

She tucked the great thing under her arm while her eyes searched for some poor hobbling old man. How quickly her feet scampered when the sight of an old, dark-skinned man bent over his stick in a lonely corner met her eyes! She startled him fiercely.

"Old man! Tell me to throw my pumpkin and pick you up!" she almost shouted.

He blinked up at her. Never in his lifetime had a woman made such a request of him. He did not answer and only turned to swat a fly.

"Say it!" she repeated.

She proved to be a persistent woman, and he even more stubborn than she was. People strolling about on that dirt path crowded around, amused at the show they were making.

"Can't you find it in your heart to please the woman?"

When his assent was finally murmured, the woman didn't wait until his words were finished. She picked him up with mannish strength and hopped about until she got home.

"Now can I go, woman?" he asked.

"Go where? No! You must say, 'Take me inside and carry me upstairs.'"

After a few refusals, he was compelled to say as she asked. That was when she threw him onto her back again and bounced him all the way up the stairs. When she dumped him on the floor again, he thought she would now let him be. Perhaps she only wanted a bit of exercise.

"Now you must say, 'Cook the pumpkin and feed me,'" she ordered.

"Pumpkin! I don't like pumpkins! Anything but that!" he protested.

But she went into her kitchen and cooked it for him anyhow. She held the smoking bowl of hot stew beneath his nose when she was done, and he shook his head adamantly.

"Please! I don't like it!"

"You must eat!"

And eat it he did, under her watchful glare. When the bowl was empty at last, he opened his mouth to say that he needed to leave but was interrupted.

"You're going to ask me to make a bed for you and put you to sleep, I suppose? Right away!"

"Sleep here? In your home? O gentle God! O Allah's Prophet!"

"I won't change my mind!"

She clapped her hands for her girls to come down, and they set to work with blankets and sheets.

"Here, you must sleep," she told him.

They covered him with heavy blankets. When they were sure that he was not going to protest and was still, they got some thick wooden rods and beat the life out of him, just like their neighbor had done, all the while thinking of the golden coins they would soon have.

When floor and man were one, the mother knelt down and slowly uncovered the blanket, bit by bit. Instead of the glimmering coins they were expecting, they were met by crawling snakes and scorpions that were ready to poison them to death!

THE ANNOYING DOVE

The molukia soup in this story is made with mallow leaves (jute leaves). You can find recipes by searching the web for "molokhia."

The daughter of the sultan was taking her bath. She was scraping her smooth skin with a body scraper that was specially made with a flowery smell and relaxing in the warm water. She heard annoying singing coming from the window. There was a dove. The dove found a golden pin on the ground and kept singing:

> *Walla Attaqeet meshkas.*
> *Walla Attaqeet meshkas.*
> *Walla Attaqeet meshkas.*
> (Which means, "I found a pin.")

The princess got very annoyed. She wanted some quiet to enjoy her bath. But this annoying dove kept singing, even after the princess admonished her to stop.

"That is it!" the princess said. "Hey, servant, send somebody to take the pin from that stupid bird. Then let us see if she has anything to sing about."

Well, they took the golden pin from her, but she kept singing:

> *Walla kadow meenni.*
> *Walla kadow meenni.*
> *Walla kadow meenni.*
> (Which means, "They took it from me.")

The princess got angry. With a red face, she ordered her servant, "Go catch this dumb animal. Let me teach her a lesson."

The dove surrendered very easily and seemed happy. She kept chanting, moving her eyebrows up and down and teasing the princess more and more, even though she was caged:

> *Walla Massaki Shater.*
> *Walla Massaki Shater.*
> *Walla Massaki Shater.*
> (Which means, "My catcher is very clever.")

The princess now got so furious. "I'll teach this wordy animal a good lesson and let her be quiet forever."

"Hey, servant, I crave *molukia* soup," the princess said with ludicrous voice. "Take this delicious bird and prepare me a good meal."

The servant brought a sharp knife and slaughtered the poor dove. Surprisingly, the dove kept singing:

> *Walla alsakeena hadda.*
> *Walla alsakeena hadda.*
> *Walla alsakeena hadda.*
> (Which means, "The knife is very sharp.")

They put her in hot water with herbs, onions, and carrots to make the broth, but she kept chanting:

> *Walla hammami dafi.*
> *Walla hammami dafi.*
> *Walla hammami dafi.*
> (Which means, "My bath is so warm.")

The broth was ready, so they added the *molukia*. The dove kept singing. The princess got more and more angry listening to her. Crunching the words from anger, the princess ordered her servant to hurry up the process and finish the soup so she could munch that noisy bird. However, the dove kept chanting:

> *Walla bustani akdar.*
> *Walla bustani akdar.*
> *Walla bustani akdar.*
> (Which means, "My garden is so green.")

After finishing preparing the tasty *molukia*, the servant served the noisy dove that refused to be silent to the princess. The princess chewed the first bite of that dove, thinking that would solve the problem. However, the dove kept singing loudly, describing the pearly teeth of the princess"

> *Walla saffain Lolo.*
> *Walla saffain Lolo.*
> *Walla saffain Lolo.*
> (Which means, "Two rows of pearls.")

The princess swallowed the dove, praying to Allah that she would stop singing. With a higher voice, the dove chanted, describing the princess's throat:

> *Woooooooooo.*
> *Walla Tobtabi Mezahlaq.*
> *Walla Tobtabi Mezahlaq.*
> *Walla Tobtabi Mezahlaq.*
> (Which means, "The tile is very slippery.")

Finally, the dove settled in the princess's stomach. Nevertheless, that did not keep her from singing. With a very loud voice so the princess could hear her, the sassy dove chanted:

> *Walla salloni wasea'.*
> *Walla salloni wasea'.*
> *Walla salloni wasea'.*
> (Which means, "I got a very spacious living room.")

The next day, while the princess kept hearing the voice of this annoying bird, she had to go the bathroom. All of the sudden, the dove came out of her in one piece, still singing her irritating songs, and flew off very far away. The dove looked back at the princess, moving her eyebrows up and down with a taunting look, and KEPT SINGING!

THE SEVEN BUCKTHORN PICKERS

Once seven girls went looking for buckthorn. They walked in the desert and looked and looked until they saw a *sidra* (buckthorn tree). The girls asked the *sidra*, "Oh, tree, do you have any buckthorns?" The tree said, "My sister who is behind me has some."

They kept walking and walking until they saw another *sidra*. They asked the tree, "Oh, tree, do you have any buckthorns?"

But the tree said, "My sister who is behind me has some."

They kept walking and walking until they saw a third *sidra*. They asked that tree, "Oh, tree, do you have any buckthorns?"

And that tree said, "Yes!"

So they stopped by the *sidra* and put their baskets down. Then they looked at each other, wondering who would climb the tree full of thorns, but none of them volunteered.

Their leader said to one of the girls, "You, with little *abaya* (mantle), go climb the *sidra*."

The girl with *abaya* said, "I fear that my *abaya* will be torn. Then my mom will punish me."

The leader said to another girl, "You, with the little *serwal* (long underpants), go climb the *sidra*."

The girl with *serwal* said, "I fear that my *serwal* will be torn. Then my mom will punish me."

The leader said to the third girl, "You, with the little *shayla* (head scarf), go climb the *sidra*."

The girl with *shayla* said, "I fear that my *shayla* will be torn. Then my mom will punish me."

The leader said to the fourth girl, "You, with the little *thobe* (long dress), go climb the *sidra*."

The girl with *thobe* said, "I fear that my *thobe* will be torn. Then my mom will punish me."

Then the leader looked at the fifth, and smallest, girl, "You, with the little *jaed* (a dress made of sheep leather), go climb the tree."

The little girl with the *jaed* knew that her dress could not be torn, so she climbed up the tree, started picking buckthorns, and throwing them to the girls until they told her their baskets were full. The little girl with *jaed* went down, took her covered-up basket, put it on her head, and went walking with the rest of the girls toward the village.

One hundred meters before they reached the village, one of the girls said, "Let's check who has the most buckthorns."

The little girl with the *jaed* looked at her basket and, to her shock, found it empty. The girls had not filled her basket up. She asked them to go back with her to pick buckthorns, as she could not go back to her family empty handed. The girls refused, as it was too late, and they left her and headed home.

The little girl with the *jaed* was now upset, but she decided to go back to the *sidra* to get her buckthorns. It was late, but she could not fail her waiting family. She reached the *sidra*, climbed it, and started picking the buckthorns, when she saw a big hideous beast.

He stopped under the tree and said with a roar, "Who is that on top of the *sidra*?"

The girl replied respectfully, "It is I, Uncle."

The ghoul said, "Throw me some buckthorns."

So the little girl picked buckthorns and threw them into the ghoul's wide-open mouth. Soon she felt tired. "Are you full now, Uncle?" she asked.

The ghoul said, "One tummy is full, the other is hungry, and the third is too wide to be full."

So the girl kept working hard picking buckthorns and throwing them into his wide-open mouth. But she felt really tired. "Are you full now, Uncle?" she called.

"One tummy is full, the other is full, but the third is too wide to be full," growled the ogre.

The poor girl kept working hard picking buckthorns and throwing them into his wide-open mouth. Yet a third time she stopped and called down, "Are you full now, Uncle?"

"The first tummy is full, the other tummy is full, and the third has had enough buckthorns! Climb on down now."

The little girl with the *jaed* climbed down, shaking with fear. The ghoul told her to gather wood sticks so he could light a big fire. The little girl kept collecting sticks and gathering them in a pile while the ghoul was digging a deeo hole in the ground. When he was done, he put the sticks in the hole and lit a big fire. The little girl was sure that he was building the fire to cook her.

"Uncle, you should look down in the hole to make sure all those sticks caught fire," she told him. And when the ghoul bent over to look down into the hole, the little girl pushed him into the fire.

The ghoul cried out, asking the girl for help, "If you help me out, I will give you what is under the white stone."

She did not respond.

"If you help me out, I will give you what is under the red stone."

No response.

"If you help me out, I will give you what is under the black."

No response.

The little girl heard a loud cry and then silence. When she looked into the hole, she saw that the ghoul was destroyed for good. She thanked God for giving her the strength to defeat the stupid ghoul, took her basket, and was about to go home when she remembered what the ghoul had said about the stones.

The girl looked for the stones he had talked about. To her surprise, she found three stones lying on the ground: white, red, and black. When she lifted the white stone, she found silver jewels. Under the red stone, she found gold jewels. And under the black stone, she found pearls and precious stones. The little girl with the *jaed* filled her basket with all she could carry and went home.

RELIGIOUS TALES

A WISE YOUNG BOY

The ruler of Rome once sent a clever man to Baghdad to challenge the wise men there. In those days, Baghdad was the capital of the Islamic Empire. It was a great center of learning and Islamic knowledge. But the Romans wanted to challenge the Muslim scholars to a debate.

The Kahlifah of Baghdad agreed to the contest. He brought together all the wisest scholars from his kingdom, and they prepared to listen to the Roman's questions.

The Roman then challenged them this way: "What was there before Allah?"

"In which direction does Allah face?

"What is Allah doing at this moment?"

Everyone was stunned. How could they answer such questions?

But one young boy whispered to his father, "I can answer these."

Everyone was shocked, but the Khalifah gave the boy the opportunity to try.

So the Roman gave his question once more.

"What was there before Allah?"

"Do you know how to count?" asked the boy.

"Yes, of course," replied the Roman.

"Then count down from ten."

The Roman counted, "Ten, nine, eight . . .." When he reached "one," he stopped.

"But what comes before 'one'?" the boy wanted to know.

"Nothing at all," replied the Roman.

"Of course," said the boy. "So if there is nothing before the number 'one,' how could there be anything before the One who is Allah?"

At this, the Roman was silenced. So he asked his second question.

"In which direction is Allah facing?"

"That is easy to answer," said the boy. "Bring me a candle."

The boy lit the candle, and the flame shown out in all directions.

"Now tell me, in which direction is the light facing?"

"Well it goes out in ALL directions, of course," replied the Roman.

"Just so. And if the flame can shine in all directions at once, why do you not believe that Allah also would not face in all directions at once?"

The Roman knew he was bested. But still he tried his third question.

But the boy spoke up. "This seems unfair. You are standing up above and asking all the questions looking down on me. It seems only right that we should switch places. Let me come up on the platform for the last question, and you should descend."

The Roman agreed to this, and they switched places. Then the Roman asked his last question.

"What is Allah doing at this moment?"

The boy laughed. "Why, at this moment, Allah has just caused a Roman who came to mock Islam to come down from the stage and look up at a mere boy who honors Islam."

The Roman was too embarrassed. He returned to Rome defeated, with news of the wisdom of even the young in Baghdad.

This boy was to grow up to become one of Islam's most famous scholars. His name was Abu Hanifah (*Rahmatullah alayhi*: May Allah have mercy on him). Imam Abu Hanifah (Imam-e-Azam) was known as the Great Imam of Islam.

THE KING, THE PRINCE, AND THE NAUGHTY SHEEP

This story is told about the historical figures King Daud and Suleiman.

There was a King Daud, or David in English, and his son Suleiman, or Solomon in English. Suleiman was able to understand the conversation between animals. He understood the conversation between fish. He understood the conversation between sheep. He understood the conversation between insects.

King Daud used to travel all over the world and take his son, Suleiman, with him because he wanted Suleiman to learn wisdom from him.

People used to come to King Daud all the time for their problems. If they had an argument, they would come to King Daud. If they had any kind of problem, they would come to King Daud. And King Daud always listened very carefully. And Suleiman would listen as well.

One day, when Suleiman was 11 years old, some men came with a problem. A shepherd and a farmer and a flock of sheep arrived. Suleiman liked the sheep very much. They had these beautiful wool coats. The sheep kept saying, "BAAAh BAAAHH," and he understood them.

The first man was furious. His face was so angry, and he talked in a very loud voice. "That man! His animals came into my garden. They ate all my fruit . . . all my plants! The carrots . . . the parsley. . . ."

King Daud turned to the shepherd. The shepherd was angry as well. The shepherd turned to the sheep and said, "So you went into this man's garden and ate his plants!"

The sheep heard this and turned and whispered to each other, "Nnn . . . nnn . . . nnn. You remember the sweet plants. . . . You remember the sweet parsley. Oh my gosh. It was sooo delicious."

Suleiman understood. He told King Daud what they had said.

So King Daud ruled. "Here is my conclusion. The plants of this farmer are ruined. And he has nothing left to eat or sell. So I judge that the man will give all the sheep to this man."

The shepherd fell down and started crying. "My life is ruined. Just ruined! What is a shepherd without sheep? What is a shepherd without sheep?"

The sheep started talking to each other. "Nnn nn . . . nnn . . . nnn. The shepherd loved us so much. How can we have brought this misfortune on our shepherd?"

Suleiman told all this to King Daud. And finally King Daud, with a big smile, said, "Now. The plants are ruined. And the farmer doesn't have anything either to sell or to eat. But he still has his own land. So if the shepherd will give all his sheep to the farmer, he won't have anything. So that is not fair too.

"The shepherd will take care of the land. He will plant the seeds. He will care for the crops. At the same time, the farmer will take care of the sheep. He will get the use of their wool. And that will pay for the lost plants. When all the vegetables and the grains are grown again, they can trade back."

The shepherd smiled. The farmer smiled a very big smile.

King Daud smiled a very big smile.

And the sheep happily returned, saying, "Bahh bahhh baahh."

THE MIRACLE OF THE SPIDER'S WEB

It happened that Prophet Mohammad was invited to Madinah. The people there valued his wisdom and faith in Allah and wanted him to come lead their city. But at that same time, the Quraysh, a tribe from Mecca, were trying to harm Prophet Mohammad. These people from Mecca did not believe in Prophet Mohammad's preaching that there was one and only one God.

As Prophet Mohammad and his friend Abu Bakr made their way to Madinah, they suddenly saw those men of Mecca approaching. Quickly they hid themselves in the Cave of Thawr. There they waited, hoping that the men from Mecca would not discover them. If they were found, they would be trapped there in the dark cave. But there was no other place to hide.

As they waited, praying, and listening for any sound of the approaching men, they saw a tiny spider emerge from a crack and begin working quickly, weaving back and forth across the cave entrance. Without stopping, the tiny spider kept working back and forth, back and forth, until the cave entrance was hung with a complete spider web.

Soon the men of Mecca came to the cave. "No use wasting time looking in there," said one. "Anyone passing would have had to break the spider web."

"True," said another. "Let's hurry on."

Abu Bakr told the Prophet, "But those are your own people searching to harm you. I am sad that something might happen to you now."

But the Prophet told him, "Don't be afraid. Allah is with us." And the actions of that tiny spider showed this to be true.

Thus Prophet Mohammad and Abu Bakr reached Madinah in safety and were welcomed by the people there. That journey the Prophet took from Mecca to Madinah is known as the Hijrah.

'UMAR IBN AL-KHATTAB COOKS FOOD
FOR HUNGRY CHILDREN

'Umar Ibn Al-Khattab (AD 579–644) was the second Caliph of Islam. He is said to have set up the first welfare state, offering relief to the poor, elderly, and disabled.

'Umar was the Caliph, and his servant was Aslam. Aslam told a story about 'Umar helping a family one night. The two had been out traveling near Madinah when they saw the light of a fire. Thinking it was some horsemen, 'Umar wanted to go see who was camped in that place. But when they came near, they realized that it was a poor woman and her children. When 'Umar questioned her, she told him that the cold and dark had forced her to spend the night in that spot. Her children were huddled together crying.

"Why are your children crying like this?" asked 'Umar.

"It is only that they are very hungry," said the old woman.

"But what are you boiling in your pot there on the fire?" 'Umar wanted to know.

"It is only water," said the old woman. "At least it will be warm in their stomachs, and perhaps they will be able to sleep. Allah alone will judge between us and 'Umar."

Of course, this woman had no idea that she was talking to 'Umar himself. She was implying that 'Umar should have been looking after them better.

'Umar was taken aback. "But how could 'Umar know about your situation?" he asked.

"Should he hold the office of Caliph if he is not aware of the condition of his people?" she replied.

At that, 'Umar took his leave, and he and Aslam went to where their supplies were stored. 'Umar took a bag of flour and some fat and asked Aslam to load them on his own back.

When Aslam offered to carry the supplies himself, 'Umar said, "But can you carry my load on the Day of Judgment? I must do this myself."

So 'Umar himself carried the flour back to the woman. He gave it to her to knead, and while she cooked, he fanned the fire for her. Aslam reported that 'Umar leaned over and blew on the fire while the woman cooked, the smoke rising through his beard. When the meal was prepared, he asked the woman to bring a platter, and he poured the food out and fanned it to cool it while the children ate.

When the family was full, 'Umar gave them the rest of the flour and fat and left.

As 'Umar and Aslam went away, the woman called after them, "Allah bless you. You are more deserving of the office of Caliph than the Amir of Muslims."

"Well, if you come to see the Amir of Muslims tomorrow, you will find me there, Allah willing," replied 'Umar. But he did not leave the place. Instead he hid at some distance and watched the children playing, until they fell asleep. Aslam thought this was not proper. But 'Umar would not leave until he had seen for himself that the children were happy and had gone to sleep.

Then 'Umar thanked Allah and went home, telling Aslam that he could not have been at ease until he saw for himself that they were happy and comfortable.

SAUDI ARABIA: OTHER TALES

Retold by Margaret Read MacDonald

MAKKI AND KAKKI

There once was a little boy named Makki who was convinced by a vendor to buy a mouse in a little cage. Makki's mother was furious to learn that he had spent his money on this. But Makki insisted that the mouse must be fed nothing but raisins and rose water and it would bring them good luck. So his mother put raisins and rose water in the little cage for the tiny creature and hung its cage from the ceiling.

That night at midnight, Makki's mother was awakened by a tiny chirping noise from the mouse cage. "Oh, mother of Makki, please answer Kakki. If Kakki needs to go, where should he leave the 'dough'?"

Makki's mother knew that Kakki the mouse was asking where he could go to the bathroom. "Just anywhere you like, little Kakki," she called.

Imagine her surprise when she awoke the next morning to find the little mouse cage full of gold coins!

Every night it was the same thing. At midnight, Kakki would begin to call out, "Oh, mother of Makki, please answer Kakki. If Kakki needs to go, where should he leave the 'dough.'?"

"Leave it right there in your cage, if you like," replied Makki's mother.

And soon Makki and his mother had enough golden coins to buy everything they had ever wanted.

Now, the nosy neighbor lady soon noticed how wealthy her next door neighbors were becoming. So she had to ask how it was that they were now so rich.

"Why it is just because of our pet mouse, Kakki," replied Makki's mother. And she told the whole story.

"Oh, please let me borrow your mouse for just one night," begged the neighbor. "I will take very good care of it."

The greedy woman stuffed the mouse with raisins and rose water, hoping it would poop a great deal. And she spread a sheet under its cage to catch the gold.

At midnight, she heard a little peeping from the mouse's cage, "Oh, neighbor, so envious indeed. Where could mousy be relieved?"

The woman was overjoyed. "Fill the cage! Cover the floor! On the table! On the bed! Even on my head if you like! Just lots and lots!"

And when she awoke in the morning, sure enough, the cage, the floor, the table, the bed, and even her head were covered . . . in mouse poop!

THE MOUSE AND THE EGGSHELL BOAT

Little Mouse was taking a walk when she found an eggshell on the ground.

"A boat! A boat! What a great boat for a mouse!"

Little Mouse carried the eggshell to the stream, jumped in, and began to row along.

Soon Rat saw her coming. "Whose boat is this?" Rat called.

"This is the boat of Mouse!"

"Well I am the Rat. Can I come aboard?"

"Why not?" answered Mouse.

So the two friends paddled downriver. Soon they came upon Yellow Chick.

"Whose boat is this?" called Yellow Chick.

"This is boat of Mouse and Rat!" called the two friends from inside their eggshell boat.

"Well I am Yellow Chick-who-likes-to-peck! Can I come aboard too?"

"Why not?" called the friends. And Yellow Chick hopped in.

Soon Rooster spotted them. "Hey! Whose boat is this?"

"This is the boat of Mouse and Rat and Yellow Chick-who-likes-to-peck!" called the three friends.

"Well I am the Cock-that-crows-on-the-deck! May I come in?"

"Come on in!" So the four drifted and paddled happily down the stream.

But then they met Big Dog. "Whose boat is this?" Dog wanted to know.

"This is the boat of Mouse and Rat and Yellow Chick-who-likes-to-peck and Cock-that-crows-on-the-deck!" shouted the happy friends.

"Well I am Dog-the-companion-of-any-trip. May I come in?"

"Come on in!" shouted the four friends.

So Dog-the-companion-of-any-trip lifted up one leg and set it down in the eggshell . . . and the entire boat collapsed and sank.

It's important to know when enough is enough.

THE CAT COUNTRY

There once was a woman who kept her house spotless and wanted everything about her to be quite prim and proper.

One day, when the woman bent over to pick up something from the floor, she burped.

"Oh my! What a shocking thing to do! Thank goodness no one heard me do that," muttered the woman. But just then the cat sitting behind her on the floor *mewed*. "Oh, the CAT heard me!

"Cat, you must promise not to tell. Here is a piece of meat. Now just don't tell anyone that you heard me burp."

The cat ate up the meat. Then the cat went, "Meow."

"Oh, you naughty cat! You still plan to tell on me? Well here is another piece of meat. Now you must not tell."

But as soon as the cat had finished that piece of meat, the cat said, "Meow."

The women kept cutting off pieces of meat and throwing them to the cat. But it was no use; the cat just kept on meowing.

The women put on her abaya and went out and stood by the front door, weeping. She was sure the cat would tell her husband about her impropriety.

An old woman passing by asked her why she was crying. When she heard about the cat and the burps, the old woman said, "You must go to the Matron of the Cats and complain about this cat of yours."

"But how do I find this Matron of the Cats?" the woman wanted to know.

The old woman gave her a ball and a stick. "Hit the ball with this stick," she told her, "and follow it wherever the ball rolls."

So the weeping woman whacked the ball with the stick and took off running after it. The ball rolled on and on, and the woman ran to keep up. After a great while, the ball came to a hole in the ground . . . and rolled right down. So the woman followed it down into the cavern. There were cats everywhere. There were cat guards and cat servants. She asked for the Matron of the Cats and was passed along until she came to a magnificent cat sitting on a throne-like chair.

The woman told all about the burp that had inadvertently popped out . . . and about the cat that ate up all the meat and still seemed to be threatening to tell.

When the Matron Cat had heard all this, she sent one of her cat servants to summon all the burps to come to her. "Which of you burps forced yourself onto this very proper lady and made her burp in front of her cat?"

One little burp came forward and sheepishly bowed. "I'm afraid it was I."

So the burp was punished severely. Then the Matron Cat gave the woman an armful of fine gifts to take home and told her it would not happen again.

When the woman came home carrying her gifts, the next door neighbor saw her coming. "Where on earth did you get all these treasures?" she wanted to know.

So the woman told her all about the burp and the cat and the Matron of the Cats.

Now the neighbor thought she knew how *she* could get presents for herself. So the next day, she drank glass after glass of water, until she too produced a small "burp." Then she grabbed her cat and squeezed it until it went, "Meow!" Then she stuffed meat into the cat, squeezed it again for another "Meow!" and stuffed more meat in. Then she raced off to find the Matron of the Cats and complain.

The Matron of the Cats sent for the burps once again.

"I am the one that she burped," admitted one of the burps. "But she drank so much water I could not do anything else. She MADE me do it."

Then the woman's cat was called. "I didn't want to eat all that meat," said the cat. "She FORCED me to eat it."

So the neighbor was rewarded all right—but not with gifts. She was given a good beating and sent back home.

THE LOST CITY OF UBAR

This tale was recounted by a man from Saudi Arabia who was visiting Kuwait.

It is said that once, long ago, a magnificent city stood in the deserts of Saudi Arabia, deep in the area called the Rub al-Kahli, the Empty Quarter. This is an enormous area of sand plains and sand dunes. Camel trains crossed the area, bringing frankincense and myrrh from Oman and Yemen north to trade. And somewhere in this desert stood Ubar. There is a fabulous tale told about Ubar.

The walls of Ubar are said to have been covered with gold and silver and encrusted with rubies. Its gardens were known as Jennat 'Ad, the Paradise of 'Ad. And beautiful ladies walked there whose bodies were as clear as crystal. This was the heavenly part of the city. In another area was a fiery furnace that served as the hell of the city.

The King of 'Ad had everything he could possibly wish for, so one day he decided to fly up to heaven and kill Allah himself. He called all of the strongest eagles in the land to come to his palace and chose the strongest one of all to carry him aloft. By holding pieces of meat out in front of the bird, he was able to control its flight.

So he climbed on the eagle's back and took off. The flight was a very long one, but two months later, he finally reached the gates of heaven. There he was stopped by some angels who asked him what he wanted up in heaven.

"I have come to find Allah," he retorted. "I plan to kill him!"

The angels were horrified. "He is down below," they misinformed him. "Go look for him there."

So King 'Ad leaned forward and tipped his stick with the meat down in front of the eagle. But he did this so suddenly that the eagle went into a steep dive. King 'Ad fell off the eagle's back.

He fell. But he fell so slowly that it took 20 years for him to reach earth. And as he fell, his body disintegrated until when it hit earth there was nothing left but his skull. And Allah caused the winds to cover that with sand and to also bury the entire city of Ubar in sand.

Years passed, and one day a wolf came upon the skull of 'Ad. What a great place to shelter from the sun! So the wolf crept into the right eye of the skull and lay down in the cool interior. Then along came a gazelle, and he stepped into the left eye of the skull to find shade also. This skull of King 'Ad was so large that neither was aware of the other.

Just then a Badawi man passed by and discovered the skull. He tapped on it with his camel stick to see if it was stone or bone. It was certainly too huge to be bone, but it looked like a man's skull.

From within the skull came a deep voice, "Have no doubts. Do not laugh."

The Badawi man was startled. He hurried to Solomon, the son of David, and told him what he had discovered. "I was riding through the desert," he said, "when I spied something that looked like a gigantic skull sticking up from the sand. When I came near, a wolf rushed out of one eye socket, and a gazelle rushed out of the other. I rapped on the skull with my cane, and a voice came out of it: 'Have no doubts. Do not laugh.'"

"Can you take me to see this strange thing?" asked King Solomon.

"I certainly can. I am a Badawi of the desert!"

"Well," said King Solomon, "if all that you say is true, I will reward you with a weight of gold equal to your own weight. But if what you say is not true, I will put you in prison for this big lie."

The Badawi man agreed, and they set off. After much traveling, they came to the giant skull. It was indeed lying there, half-buried in the sand.

But when King Solomon struck the skull with his stick, not a sound came from it. He tapped again. Silence. The Badawi man rapped hard on the skull. Still not a sound.

So King Solomon ordered his servants to put the man in jail.

As soon as the Badawi man was in jail, a voice came from the skull. "Didn't I tell you? 'Have no doubts. Do not laugh at me.'"

Now King Solomon was sorry that he had ordered the poor Badawi imprisoned. He called all of the birds of the air and asked them if they knew anything about a king called 'Ad ibn Gin'ád. But the birds had never heard of such a king or such a kingdom.

At long last, a very old eagle arrived. This eagle was so old that the feathers had all fallen from its aged body. King Solomon asked this eagle if he had ever heard of a king called' Ab ibn Gin'ád and a city of silver and gold called Ubar.

"If you can tell me about this king and this place, I will run my hand over your aged body and make all of your feathers grow back. You will become as a young bird once more."

The eagle bowed and said, "Indeed, I do know of the 'Ad ibn Gin'ád, and I can take you to the place where the city of Ubar lies hidden under the sands."

So King Solomon ran his hand over all of the eagle's featherless body, and new feathers grew. He was like a young bird again. Then he led King Solomon and his entourage across the sands for a very long way, and at last the eagle came to rest on a spot of sand.

"Here is the place," said the eagle. "Beneath all this sand lies the lost city of Ubar."

So King Solomon called up shimál, the northwest wind. And it came in a mighty dust storm. Then he called up kaus, the southeast wind, and it too blew a dust storm. Then he called on gharbi, the west wind, and sharqi, the east wind. And all of these winds blew and blew and blew . . . and gradually the lost city of Ubar began to emerge from beneath the sands.

Then King Solomon saw for himself the great palace of gold and silver and rubies. He saw the beautiful gardens and the fiery furnace. And seeing all of these amazements, he was afraid that people might get seduced by the wealth and become arrogant He feared they might end up like 'Ab ibn Gin'ád. So he called the winds to blow again. And the shimál, the kaus, the gharbi, the sharqi all blew about until the city was covered once more and no one could tell where it might have lain.

To this day, the lost city of Ubar remains hidden beneath the desert sands . . . somewhere in the Rub al-Khali, the Empty Quarter of Arabia.

FOLKTALES FROM BAHRAIN

AZIZ, SON OF HIS MATERNAL UNCLE

Bu-Zaid's sister had six sons and a daughter by her husband and a youngest son by another union. She called him "Aziz, Son of His Maternal Uncle." Bu-Zaid asked his sister to lend him a son to help on his quest for the maiden Alya. She gave him her first son. He took the son into the desert, and when their rations and water ran out after several days, he said to this boy, "Serve me coffee." Then Bu-Zaid went to sleep.

There was neither fire nor water available. When Bu-Zaid woke up, he found no coffee. In anger, he hit the boy and killed him. Then he returned to his sister and asked for another son.

Bu-Zaid repeated the same actions with this boy. And with the next and the next, until only the youngest son was left. He took Aziz into the dessert, and they traveled for several days, until their water and supplies had all run out. Then Bu-Zaid told Aziz, "Make me coffee." And Bu-Zaid went to sleep.

It was midday, and there was no firewood and no water. Aziz took his own she-camel and ran it until it sweated. Then he collected the sweat and placed it in the coffee pot. He cut off the saddle ropes and set them on fire. When Bu-Zaid awoke, the coffee was ready.

Bu-Zaid realized that this Aziz, unlike his brothers, was a man capable of enduring hard times.

So Bu-Zaid set off for the country of Alya, with Aziz as companion. When they finally arrived, after much hard traveling, they heard drumming and saw dancing in the streets of the royal city. Alya, the sultan's daughter, was to be married to her cousin that very day.

"How can I obtain that girl?" wondered Bu-Zaid.

"Uncle, you have grown old," said Aziz. "I will bring her for you."

"We will make ourselves into wandering poets," said Aziz. Aziz was a very handsome youth, and his uncle was dark-skinned. They dressed as poets and stood under the window and chanted.

Soldiers came and demanded what they were doing. "We are poets!" said Aziz. And he began to sing with the most beautiful voice.

Alya looked out her window to see what was going on. She was dressed in her wedding gown and looked so lovely. When she saw Aziz and heard his beautiful singing, she fell in love with him! She nodded to the guard to let Aziz and his uncle enter. To her father, she begged, "Father, allow these poets to enter. There is no proscription against poets coming to sing for us." Her father agreed, but said that only one could enter. So Aziz came in.

Then the old woman who guarded the girls said, "O, Alya's playmates, depart away from her. For a lion came for her from the farthest distance."

So her girlfriends all left her alone with Aziz.

Aziz called to his uncle outside. "I will lower her to you with a rope."

Alya was ready to go with him, but she said, "What about my cousin, whom I just married?"

"I will take your place in the wedding bed," said Aziz.

So they exchanged clothing, and Alya was lowered out of the window to Bu-Zaid. And Aziz lay down on the wedding bed.

When the groom came in, Aziz turned his back to him. So the groom moved to the other side of the bed. Aziz turned his back to him. So the groom moved back to the other side of the bed. Aziz turned his back on him. And so it went for some time. But at last Aziz dozed off. Then the groom pulled back the veil and saw Aziz's face. "This is a MAN!"

He roused the household shouting, "You, Alya's family! This is not Alya! This is a MAN!"

Her mother came running. "Do not tread on our honor," she said.

Then she thought and added, "Cut off one of Alya's braids. Make a small wound on her leg. In the morning we will see if Alya has these marks."

So the groom cut off one of the braids of Aziz, who had long hair himself. And he wounded Aziz in his leg with a knife.

Aziz woke in the morning to find his braid chopped off and a small wound in his leg. He realized that he had been marked. He lowered himself through the window and hurried to Bu-Zaid. "Quick, cut off one of Alya's braids and make a small cut on her leg." They did this and then returned her to her room.

Alya's father was returning with the groom to check on the bride. "If what you claim is not true, I will kill you!" muttered the angry father. There was Alya lying on the bed, with one braid cut off and a wound on her leg. So that was the end of the groom.

That night Aziz returned and lowered Alya out the window once more. Then the three made their way toward the country of Aziz and Bu-Zaid. But on the way, they came to a spring. Bu-Zaid lowered a bucket for water, but the bucket fell. He wanted to go down into the well to get it, but Aziz said, "Uncle you have grown old. I will go down."

Now Aziz did not realize this, but the wound on his leg must never touch water. He went into the spring and got the bucket with the water, but a bit of water sloshed onto his wound. And so the story ends sadly, as Aziz sickened and died.

When Bu-Zaid reached home without Aziz, the mother of Aziz cried, "Where is my son?"

"Before I tell you," said Bu-Zaid, "go fetch a pot from a home whose walls have never been touched by grief. Go now and look for one."

The mother went to all of the tribal homesteads. She was gone traveling and looking for months. When she finally returned, Bu-Zaid asked her, "Did you find a household that has not been touched by grief? Did you get the pot?"

"No," she replied. "There is no household which has not been touched by grief."

"And neither is yours," replied Bu-Zaid. "Aziz has died."

THE SPRINGS OF BAHRAIN

Bahrain was always known for its beautiful freshwater springs. These natural springs appeared both under the sea and on land. These springs were unusual on this dry Arabian Peninsula, and Bahrain families loved to bring their children to play in them.

A legend tells that these springs were caused by stars falling from the heavens. The stars broke holes in the ground which filled up with sparkling, heavenly water.

However, nowadays, many wells have been dug in Bahrain, and the groundwater is drained. So these beautiful springs are now dry.

Kuwaiti tents erected beneath power lines. An escape from city life. Photo by Margie Deemer.

Ladies walk by the sea in Kuwait. Traditionally Kuwaiti women wear black garments covering their persons when out of the home. More modest women cover their faces with a veil as well. Photo by Margie Deemer.

Banana vendor waits by a Kuwaiti roadside, sheltered by a billboard advertising a restaurant.

Traditional forms of architecture are used in modern buildings in Kuwait City. Photo by Margie Deemer.

Fishing boats, Faheel, Kuwait. Photo by Margie Deemer.

Men's clothing vendor in Kuwait City. Photo by Margie Deemer.

FOLKTALES FROM KUWAIT

ABOUT JOUHA

Jouha tales are told throughout the Middle East. His name varies from region to region. Salma Khadra Jayyusi tells us that Juha is sometimes believed to have been Abu'l-Ghusn Dujain bin Thabit of the Fazara tribe, a person who lived in the 10th century.

In Turkey, similar stories are told about Khoja Nasruddin al-Rumi, who was born in 1208 and died in 1284 in a village in Anatolia. A Turkish friend told me he had visited the tomb of Khoja Nasruddin. The tomb had an enormous gate that was locked. However, there were no side fences, so he just walked around behind the gate to explore the tomb. It felt like a very visible final Khoja joke.

Here are three Jouha stories from Kuwait. For a Jouha story from Saudi Arabia, see page 7. For Jouha tales from Oman, see pages 50 and 52.

ANSWERING THE SCHOLAR

Once a famous scholar came to Jouha's town. He challenged anyone to try and compete against him. His challenge was this: "I will ask 40 questions. You must give the same answer to all 40 questions."

Jouha considered this easy enough. "State your questions," Jouha said.

When the questions had all been put forth, Jouha said, "I have one answer for all 40 of your questions. My answer is, 'I don't know.'"

JOUHA SINGS FROM THE MINARET

An imam of the mosque sings the call to prayer from the minaret tower five times a day. Someone with a fine voice is usually given this privilege.

One day Jouha went to the public bath. He ended up alone in there, so he started singing. His voice echoed so beautifully off the marble floors and walls. He was very proud of his magnificent singing voice. As soon as he had finished his bath, he went up to the top of the minaret at the mosque and began to sing of the glory of Allah. But his voice was so horrible that everyone came running to stop the racket.

"Jouha come down at once!" they demanded. "Your voice is atrocious."

"Just prepare me a bath up here," responded Juha, "and you will be amazed at how beautiful my voice really is."

A contemporary mosque in Kuwait. Notice the very tall minarets. The call to prayer still issues forth from these minarets six times daily.

COUNTING THE DAYS OF RAMADAN

Muslims must fast during the entire month of Ramadan. A lunar month is around 30 days long.

To keep track of the days of fasting during Ramadan, Jouha dropped a stone in a jar each day. His little daughter saw him doing that and began to drop many stones in the jar herself.

One day he was asked, "How many days remain in Ramadan, Jouha?"

"I'll count up and see how many have passed," replied Jouha. And he got out his jar of stones.

When he counted them he found 120 stones! "I can't possibly tell them this," he thought. "It sounds like way too many days."

So he made up a number. "Forty days have passed so far this month," he told them.

Everyone started to laugh at him.

"Let them laugh," he said to himself. "What would they have thought if I had told them the REAL number of days that have passed? When you are fasting, Ramadan seems to go on forever."

CHOICES

A woman once went to the tyrant Al-Hajjaj, who had captured her brother, son, and husband and was holding them for execution. The woman stood wailing and wailing at the palace gates. At last Al-Hajjaj heard her and sent for her to be brought before him.

"Why do you wail and wail at my palace gates?" he wanted to know.

"You are holding prisoner three men of my family. You have my brother, my son, and my husband. These are the last three men of our family. What can we do with no man left to us?"

Al-Hajjaj was known for his cruelty and ruthless manner, but he did feel some pity for this woman's plight. "I will grant you a boon, then," he said. "You may choose the life of one of these three. But you must choose which to save."

Immediately, the woman spoke. "Give me my brother."

Al-Hajjaj was amazed at this. "Why did you not choose your son, or your husband?"

The woman replied, "Another son can be born. Another husband can be found. A brother would be lost forever."

And when Al-Hajjaj asked what she meant by this, she explained, "I am young and can bear another son. I am attractive and can find another husband. But I can never replace a lost brother."

All-Hajjaj understood her wisdom. He said to her, "Take your brother and go."

THE HELPFUL DOG

This is retold from a story collected by folklorist Hasan M. El-Shamy. The story was told in August 1970 by Ruqayyah B., a 59-year-old former slave of African heritage living in Kuwait.

There were once three sisters who were very, very poor.

Their father brought home some meat and put it in the pot over the fire. But not waiting for the meat to finish cooking, each of the older daughters went and took meat from the pot and ate it. They kept reaching in and taking more and more until the youngest daughter grabbed the pot in anger and ran out with it. Her father and the two sisters chased after her. But she outran them, and her little dog ran off with her.

At last the girl sat down against the wall of the palace and fell asleep with exhaustion.

Along came the prince in his carriage drawn by six horses. "Who is this beautiful girl sleeping beside my palace?"

The prince had the girl and her dog taken into the palace, and he asked that she be dressed in fine clothing. When he saw how very beautiful she was now, he insisted on marrying her. At first his father, the king, objected. But in the end the prince got his way.

Now the girl and her little dog lived so happily in the palace with the king.

But one day when she was sitting with the prince, she remembered her days of poverty and laughed.

"Why do you laugh?" asked the prince.

"Because your beard reminded me of the broom in my father's house."

The prince showed offense at this, so the girl quickly lied. "That broom is made of gold and pearl beads."

The girl now feared that the prince might learn the truth about her family. But the little dog said, "Don't worry. I will find a way for you to fool him."

Sometime later, the dog said, "I have been searching, and I found a rich man who is dying. He has just confessed to his family that he has a daughter from another wife. As soon as he dies, you must go and tell them that you are his daughter."

The girl did just as the dog advised her, and the family accepted her without question. Now she had a respectable family to present to the prince as her family. When the prince came to visit them, he did indeed see a broom there that was made of gold and pearl beads.

The dog now decided to test the girl's love for him. He pretended to be sick. And the girl ignored him and just told the servants to take him down to the kitchen and keep the sick dog there. Then the dog pretended to be dead, and the girl just told the servants to toss his body out.

At that, the dog came to her and chided her. "I cannot believe you would treat me in this unfeeling way after all that I have done for you," said the dog. And he went on to inform her that he was in fact a man whom a sorceress had bewitched to take a dog's form.

Then the dog took his revenge on the unfeeling girl by going straight to the prince and telling him the secret of her upbringing. Furious that the girl had been lying to him, the prince had her sent down to the kitchen as a maid. Now in old, raggedy clothes, she had to cook and clean and scrub the floors.

At this time, the dog did indeed become sick. Now the girl took care of him tenderly. She brought food to him and sat beside him to cheer him. And when the dog did die, the girl took her clothes from her clothes chest and had the dear dog put inside. She refused to have his body thrown out.

Now the prince was missing his wife, and finally he went down to the kitchen and told her he would now forgive her. The girl was so happy. But she said she could not leave the kitchen without saying good-bye to the body of her dead dog. When she opened the chest, to their surprise, they found not a dog's body, but a dog of solid gold with large gems for eyes.

The girl and the prince lived their lives in happiness and contentment after that. And the girl was always kind to animals, especially to dogs.

THE BLACK PEARL AND THE WHITE PEARL

Kuwait lies adjacent to Iraq, so the city of Baghdad is an important nearby city. The nearby country of Bahrain is known for its pearl fishermen. The wealthier people of the Arabian Peninsula owned slaves brought from Tanzania and elsewhere in Africa. Many of these slaves obtained their freedom and entered professions, such as pearl diving. This story was heard in Kuwait by H. R. P. Dickson and published in 1949 in his book The Arab of the Desert. *Pearl fishing was an important occupation in both Kuwait and Bahrain at that time.*

Long, long ago, in the days when Baghdad was the center of the pearl trade, there lived a beautiful princess, the daughter of the Kahlifah. This princess possessed a wondrous large black pearl, a gift from her father. It was her most highly prized possession. Every day, she would take up this large pearl and stare into it. She would stroke its lustrous surface. And one day it came into her head that she would like to have a second pearl to match it. Two perfect black pearls, just alike.

The princess sent for the city's most-experienced pearl merchant and asked if he could acquire such a pearl for her.

"In all the world, there would not be another pearl as fine as yours," he declared. "It is impossible."

But the princess kept asking him if he could not find someone who could bring her such a pearl. She would not give up on her idea.

One day, the pear seller came to the palace with news. "A pearl diver from Bahrain has just arrived in the city," he told her. "This young man is the son of a famous pearl diver. His father is now dead. But the son might know of a pearl like you desire."

"Bring him to me at once!" ordered the princess. And the young man was brought into the palace. He was a handsome young man, tall, broad-shouldered, and with such a pleasing face. The man's name was 'Anad bin Faraj.

"I have here a pearl incomparable. But I wish to obtain a match for it. Can you bring me a pearl identical to this one?"

'Anad came close to examine the pearl the princess held. "I know this pearl," he said. And a sad look came over his face. "My father brought up this pearl from a cavern deep in the sea. That cave is inhabited by a giant octopus. It means death for any who attempt to take oysters from that cave. My father was too brave. Your father, the great Khalifah, had asked for a large black pearl for his daughter. And my father vowed to find such a pearl.

"My father dove deep that day and located a single, huge oyster. He grasped it tightly in his hand and started to rise, but the giant octopus was waiting. It wrapped him in its clutches and squeezed the life from him. When his body was pulled back into the boat, his hand was still clutched tight . . . around an enormous oyster. And when that oyster was pried open . . . the pearl you now hold in your hands lay inside."

The princess was fascinated by 'Anad and his story. She asked him to come to her the next day and tell him more. This time, he was ushered into the princess's quarters. She offered him a seat on her soft couch, had refreshments brought for him, and sitting down beside him, she plied him with questions. "Would it truly be impossible for a diver to bring another pearl from that site?" she queried.

"It would indeed be death to any diver who attempted this," replied 'Anad.

Still the princess kept inviting 'Anad to the palace. She kept pleading with him to find some way to bring her the large black pearl that would match the one she already owned. On his third visit to the palace, the princess sat close to him and suddenly let loose her veil, revealing her beautiful, large, soft eyes. "For these two eyes, my brave 'Anad, would you not dare to dive near the octopus just once?"

'Anad was struck by her beauty and mesmerized by those dark eyes. He fell into a dream state in her presence. When she bent over him and pleaded, "For me will you bring it?" 'Anad could no longer resist.

"The pearl merchant has said that no two pearls in this world are alike and that your black pearl cannot be matched. But when I look into your eyes, I see two of the most perfect pearls imaginable. And they are perfectly matched. A pair. For the sake of those two matchless pearls, I will brave the monster. And with the help of Allah, I will bring you the black pearl you so desire."

"'Anad, if you succeed in this quest, your heart's desire will be given you. Even if it is half of my father's kingdom."

'Anad returned then to his homeland of Bahrain, the land of superb pearl divers and rich pearl-oyster beds. He prepared everything for his daring attempt. On a clear, calm day, 'Anad and five companions went out in their boat to the place where the dangerous cavern lay under the sea.

'Anad took a long, sharp dagger. He tied a rope around his waist and left one end in the hands of his companions. Immediately, if they felt him tug on the rope, they were to pull him up.

He fastened his wooden nose clip, held onto a rope for lowering, and stood on a stone fastened to the rope. This would keep the rope on the seashore bottom. Slowly his men let him down into the sea. Down and down and down . . . he passed the branches of gigantic corals of every hue . . . he reached the oyster shoals on the sea bottom and began to search.

And there was the cave. Dark and foreboding. But he knew he had to enter, for the largest oysters were said to grow in its dark interior. Carefully he entered the cave . . . so many oysters there . . . so large . . . but at last! The largest oyster of all! Just the kind to hold a very large pearl.

'Anad cut the oyster from its rock and reached to tug on the rope for his haul up. But the giant octopus had been lurking and slowly oozing itself out of its cave. Suddenly it wrapped a tentacle around the arm of 'Anad and began to pull him close. He yanked on the rope! He stabbed the octopus in the eye! The octopus sucked him toward it! 'Anad stabbed again and again . . . until he lost consciousness.

When he awoke, 'Anad was lying in the bottom of the boat. His friends were working frantically to revive him. 'Anad gave thanks to Allah for his survival. And then he looked down. Clasped in his hand was the huge oyster. Quickly he pried it open and . . . there in the oyster's quivering flesh lay a stunning black pearl. The exact mate to the pearl owned by the princess.

A month later, 'Anad arrived at the palace of the princess in Baghdad and asked for an audience with the princess. He was received at once and taken into the innermost reception chamber of her quarters. This time, the princess received him unveiled. She was even more beautiful than he had imagined.

"Welcome my brave 'Anad! Welcome a thousand times!" she cried with outstretched arms. "The pearl? Did you bring it?"

'Anad knelt before her and pressed both of her hands to his lips in worship and servitude. "Yes," he said simply. "Your servant has brought what you asked."

The princess took the pearl from him and lifted 'Anad to his feet. "Come and sit by me and tell me all of your adventure," she said. And they sat together for some time while 'Anad told her all that had happened, and while the princess praised him for his bravery.

Then the princess spoke. "'Anad it is time to reward you. Ask whatever is your heart's desire and it will be yours. For you too are a black pearl without price. And you have served me well, even at risk of your own life."

After a long silence, the poor pearl diver spoke. "Oh, princess, I have come to worship and love you above all things in heaven or earth. You are truly the most matchless pearl in the world. My only wish would be to ask your hand in marriage. But a white pearl such as you can never wed a humble black pearl such as I."

And so saying, this handsome son of African ancestors drew his dagger and plunged it into his heart.

Violet Dickson Talks about the Kuwaiti Pearl Fishers

Violet Dickson, the wife of H. R. P. Dickson, the man who wrote down this story, talks about the local pearl fishers when she first lived in Kuwait in the 1930s and 1940s:

> I always used to enjoy the singing of a spring evening, when the pearling fleet was in. The crews would sit on their boats, which were pulled up in front of our house, and sing their pearling songs away into the night, when we would already have gone up to sleep on the roof or often when we were having dinner up there.

She also describes the long voyages the Kuwaiti boats used to take:

> They would go on long voyages to India, East Africa, Zanzibar. I think the first year we came to Kuwait there were about 400 boats which went out. They would start in September, calling at Basra for dates, then going down to India, discharging the dates, taking another cargo across to East Africa, and then down to the Rufiji River. The winds brought them back up about the beginning of April. They laid up these big deep-sea boats, and they had just about two months with their wives before they went out again on the 15th of June. Then they went off to the pearl banks and didn't come back till the 26th or 27th of September and then off to Basra to get dates and then off again.

Source: William Tracy, "A Talk with Violet Dickson," *Saudi Aramco World* (November/December 1972): 13–19.

KILL THE MAN WHO KILLED THE DOG

This is a Badu folktale from Kuwait. H. R. P. Dickson retells this story in The Arab of the Desert (1949). He heard the story twice. Once from K. B. Mulla Sáleh, wazir to four consecutive rulers of Kuwait, and once from Othmán ibn Humaid al'Utaibi, a leader among the 'Utaiba tribe.

There once lived an old Mutairi Badawi who had three grown sons. The sons lived with their mother and father, together in one tent, and the sons helped tend their father's sheep and camels. One summer, they were encamped by a group of wells, and their closest neighbor in that encampment was a poor shepherd who owned only 10 sheep and 2 camels.

A man of their tribe came to the poor shepherd's tent one day, and the shepherd's sheep dog rushed out, snarling and barking at him. The man took his rifle and callously shot the dog dead. There was much indignation among the people at this because a sheep dog is essential to someone living in a tent. The sheep dog, called a *kalb*, drives off wolves who might attack the sheep and also keeps away thieves who might come in the night.

The three sons went to their father and told him of this outrage. It is an ages-old desert law that a man's most sacred duty is to protect his neighbor. And Prophet Mohammad himself stressed this.

"This man has killed our neighbor's dog!" his sons told their father. "It was merely barking, and he shot it. What should we do?"

The old man thought about this carefully. Then he replied, "Kill the man who killed the dog."

The sons thought their father was getting dotty to suggest such a thing. Instead, they consoled the poor shepherd who had lost his dog and spoke ill of the man who had done this thing.

A short time later, while the poor shepherd was watering his small flock of sheep at one of the wells, a gang of wild young Badu who were bringing their camels to drink pushed the shepherd aside, beat him, and broke his *haudh* (leather watering trough). This too was an unpardonable offense among the desert people.

The poor shepherd returned to his tents complaining. "Why are the strong allowed to bully the weak in this way? Is there no justice in the Mutairi tribe?"

The three sons went again to their father. They told him that their neighbor had been abused once again. "What should we do?" they asked.

The father replied swiftly this time. "Kill the man who killed the dog."

"Our father is surely becoming old and foolish," said the sons. "We aren't concerned with a dog now, but with bullies who beat this man up." They told everyone of the misbehavior of those young toughs.

But the young gang just bragged. "Of course the weak should give way to the strong. That is the law of the desert!"

Sometime after that, a junior shaikh of the tribe needed a lamb for a party he was giving. He sent his men out to buy one. But when they noticed a lamb at the tent of the poor shepherd, they just took it without payment. "This is the man who dared to complain because Arabs watered their camels before him," they told themselves. And thus they justified taking his lamb.

Now the tribe was in an uproar. It was clear that this poor shepherd was being singled out for abuse. But the shaikh for whom the lamb was stolen was powerful, with many retainers. No one wanted to start a blood feud with him over such a small matter. "Better to leave the settlement to God, who arranges everything," they said.

The three sons went once more to their father. The father was angry now. He said sharply to them, "If you had followed my advice, this would not have happened. If you want to stop this bullying and this preying upon the weak, you need to do what I told you in the first place. Kill the man who killed the dog."

So the three sons found the man who had killed the dog and killed him.

The tribe accepted this act of retribution as a just one. The relatives of the dead man said that no blood money was due them for the act. And they compensated the poor shepherd so he could purchase another sheep dog. The tough gang brought the shepherd a new *haudh* to water his sheep. And the shaikh sent three lambs to replace the one taken without payment.

Now peace and quiet was found throughout this Badu camp. Respect and fear now filled the minds of those who might be inclined to persecute the weak. This was the kind of justice that the desert dweller appreciates.

A contemporary shepherd with his sheep in Kuwait. The head scarf protects the man from sun, wind, and blowing sand.

NESÓP AND THE SNAKE

This folktale was told to H. R. P. Dickson while camped at Araifjan, April 1, 1953, by Amsha, wife of Salim al Muzaiyin.

A man named Nesóp was once traveling in the desert when he noticed a snake quivering with cold under a bush. Even though the snake was poisonous, Nesóp took pity on the poor creature. He picked it up and put it inside his *zibún* (his undergarment) to warm it. The snake lay comfortably on Nesóp's warm stomach, and after a while, its life came back to it. And in time the weather warmed.

Nesóp opened his clothing and told the snake to come out now. "The sun has warmed everything up, dear snake. It is safe for you to return to the ground and continue on your way."

But the snake said, "No, I *like* it lying in here on your warm belly. I plan to stay right here. No way will I be coming out."

Nesóp begged the snake to leave, but the snake just snarled, "If you even touch me to remove me, I will bite you!" And as this was a poisonous snake, Nesóp had no option but to let it stay where it was, close to his skin.

Nesóp went to the home of Al Husni, the fox. The fox was known for his wisdom in settling difficult matters. "I picked up this snake, when it was dying of cold," Nesóp told Al Husni, the fox. "And now the snake refuses to leave from its warm place on my belly. The snake threatens to bite me with its poisons if I even try to remove it. Can you resolve this matter?"

"Well, we will have to have a court hearing," said Al Husni, the fox. "Both of you must stand before me. And I, as judge, will decide the matter."

So the snake crawled out from Nesóp's clothing and lay on the ground before the fox.

"I have heard Nesóp's side of the matter already," said the fox. "Now what is your story, snake?"

"I am very comfortable residing inside Nesóp's warm clothing," said the snake. "Why should I be asked to give up such a warm home?"

Al Husni, the fox, turned to Nesóp. "Well, you have heard the snake's argument," said the fox. "Now what do you propose to do about it?"

"Only THIS!" shouted Nesóp. And with his *mugwar* (club-headed stick), he whopped the snake on the head and did it in.

And thus ended the court hearing and this story.

THE *HATTÁB* (WOODCUTTER) AND THE *KHAZNAH* (TREASURE)

This folktale was told to H. R. P. Dickson by Háji Abdullah al Fathil in camp on January 7, 1935.

There was once a poor woodcutter who had a wife, a family of children, and a donkey. He owned very little other than his donkey. He made his living digging up dry shrubs and taking them into the town to sell.

One Friday, he heard the preacher in the mosque talking about faith. If a man had enough faith, this wise man told the congregation, they would not have to do anything at all, and yet all good things would come to them.

The woodcutter liked this thought. He decided to stop working so hard and just trust in God. His wife was soon desperate. The woodcutter refused to go out and work. He just sat at home and proclaimed, "God will provide."

One day two young men came by en route to the desert for a hawking expedition. They asked if they could hire the woodcutter's donkey, as he wasn't using it. He gladly agreed. Now the woodcutter showed his wife the five silver coins the men had given him as payment for hiring his donkey. "See? It is just as the preacher said. God will provide." His wife was skeptical. But she did make good use of the coins to lay in provisions for the family.

The two young men were on their trip for five days and then one night. As they started heading toward home, they stopped to make a fire for the night, and scraping sand away from a spot to prepare their fire, they struck something hard. Digging in the sand, they unearthed a large wood box. It turned out to be full of gold.

They loaded it on the donkey's back and headed for town. But they dared not just ride into town with a huge box of gold, lest someone question them about it. So they made plans to sneak the gold into the town after dark and hide it in their homes. But first they needed to have supper. So one man stayed with the donkey and the gold, while the other went into the town and brought back food for their meal. The man who was left with the gold soon decided he wanted all of this and prepared to shoot his companion when he returned.

As soon as the man came back with the food, he was murdered. Then the murderer sat down to eat the food his friend had brought back from town for their evening meal.

But his friend had decided that *he* wanted all of the gold for himself, and so he had poisoned the food. Soon the murderer too lay dead.

After a while, the confused donkey just walked off and went home.

When the poor woodcutter heard his donkey bumping its head on his door, he opened it and was amazed to see a huge wooden box on the donkey's back. "Come, wife, and help me get this box off of our donkey."

They opened it and found the box was full of golden coins! "We must go and report this to the authorities at once," said the wife. "This gold does not belong to us."

"I am not so sure about that," said the woodcutter. "Remember what the preacher said. 'You need do nothing. If you have faith, God will provide.' I had great faith, and God has provided."
So the woodcutter and his wife buried the gold under their own floor. And using a little here and a little there, they were able to live for a very long time. The woodcutter kept his faith in God. And he never worked again.

Fishing boats, Faheel, Kuwait. Photo by Margie Deemer.

Palm grove near beach, Salalah, Oman. Photo by JonLee Joseph.

Flame Tree, Salalah, Oman. Photo by JonLee Joseph.

Author Margaret Read MacDonald with participants at a storytelling workshop in Kuwait.
Photo from Margaret Read MacDonald.

View from the Museum of Islamic Art, Doja, Qatar. Photo by Margaret Read MacDonald.

Door of Sultan's palace in Salalah. He now resides most of the time in a larger palace in Muscat. Photo by JonLee Joseph.

Bulbul birds in Kuwait. Photo by Margie Deemer.

Camels in the jebel ("mountains") near Salalah, Oman, return to their home pasture after the spring monsoon rains green the fields. Photo by JonLee Joseph.

Crossing the jebel. Photo by JonLee Joseph.

Unusual rooftop architecture mimics traditional pigeon houses. Villa in Kuwait. Photo by Margie Deemer.

Camping in the Kuwaiti desert. Photo by Margie Deemer. March 2013.

Omani Bedouin family of Abdullah Salim Al-Hammer at home. Woman cannot be photographed so are not in this picture. Photo by JonLee Joseph.

Proud Omani camel owner. Photo by JonLee Joseph.

Contributor JonLee Joseph with camels near Salalah, Oman. Photo from JonLee Joseph.

Mother camel named Samhahn (Good Life) near Salalah, Oman. Note red bag to protect her milk. Photo by JonLee Joseph.

Dove in Kuwait. Photo by Margie Deemer.

FOLKTALES FROM OMAN

ABU NAWAS, THE TRICKSTER

This story was collected by JonLee Joseph from Mahbrook Massan in his desert camp on the edge of the Empty Quarter on the evening of September 12, 2010. Mahbrook is a leader in the Shisr community and maintains this camp for visitors in the desert some miles from Shisr. Shisr is the site of archeological remains believed by some to be the lost city of Ubar, much searched for by archeologists over the years.

Abu Nawas is a trickster/fool whose stories are told throughout the Middle East. This tale has several Abu Nawas adventures strung together.

There was a time when Abu Nawas was crossing a desert and was very, very thirsty. This was at a time when animals and humans could speak to each other. He saw a leopard.

"Abu Nawas," said the leopard, "you can put your head inside my body. Then you can see where water is to be found. There will be a place with bitter water, a place with so-so water, and a place with sweet water."

Abu Nawas was ready to do just what the leopard told him.

"But, Abu Nawas," warned the leopard, "whatever you do . . . after you have finished drinking the water, DO NOT look up!"

Abu Nawas put his head inside the leopard. Then he saw all three drinking places. He went right to the one with sweet water. But after he finished drinking, he was hungry. So, he looked up. There were two large things hanging inside the leopard. So, Abu Nawas ate one. It was an organ of the leopard. So, the leopard crawled off to die, with Abu Nawas still inside of him.

At that time, it began to rain in the desert. This softened the dead body of the leopard so that Abu Nawas could crawl out. He then traveled on to a wadi.

In the wadi, women were tending their goats. Other women had invited the women to a festival, and they wanted to go. So, Abu Nawas said that he would take care of the goats while they went to the festival.

The women put on their best dresses and gold jewelry and went off to the celebration. Suddenly Abu Nawas had a vision. He saw a river of white and a river of red. So Abu Nawas milked all the goats, creating the river of white. Then he killed all the goats, creating the river of red blood.

After a while, one of the women came back. Horrified, she called to the other women, "Abu Nawas has killed all our goats." Because the women were far off, they could not hear her.

"What did you say?" they shouted.

So, Abu Nawas called out to the other women.

"She said you should leave your gold jewelry there for Abu Nawas!" So they did. Abu Nawas gathered up the gold jewelry and traveled on.

He traveled on until he came to a tree. He hung all the gold jewelry on the tree and then climbed up into it. Eventually, a camel caravan of six merchants came by. They were astounded by the tree hung with gold jewelry. Abu Nawas explained that the tree grew the jewelry. They arranged a trade. Abu Nawas would be given the camels and their goods; the merchants would be given the tree that would blossom with gold. Abu Nawas took the gold jewelry down from the tree and rode off on the camels with their goods. The merchants sat down under the tree to await the blossoming of more gold jewelry. They are still waiting.

And Abu Nawas is still creating more stories!

A DJINN STORY

This folktale was told to Kiera Anderson and JonLee Joseph in Arabic by Mahbrook Massan on November 28, 2012 in the Empty Quarter, close to Wubar, in Oman. It was translated into English by Kiera Anderson.

One evening, three Bedouin men were sitting in the desert around a fire. It was night, and the night sky was full of stars and the moon. They were drinking *gowha* (coffee) and talking.

Suddenly, a small child appeared. He approached the men. They welcomed him to the fire and offered a cup of *gowha*. He answered them in an adult man's voice. They marveled at this and asked him how this came to be. The young child said that he was a djinn.

He drew two lines in the sand and said, "Let me take you to the Sheik of the djinns. He took the hand of one man, and the others followed, crossing the double lines. The child introduced them to the Sheik.

Sitting beside the Sheik was a very beautiful woman. One man fell in love with her. He told her that she was the most beautiful woman in the world, and he wanted to marry her. She told him to ask her father, the Sheik.

He did ask the Sheik, who said, "Yes, but don't make her angry, whatever you do." If the man did, she would return to live with the Sheik in the Land of Djinns.

So, the man and woman married and returned to his home in the desert. Soon, a child was born. One evening, the man's father and mother, his wife, the man, and his baby boy were sitting around the fire. The wife took the baby and gently placed him in the fire. The baby boy disappeared. The man and his mother and father were horrified. The man was angry and sad but did not say anything.

Several days later, the man had to work out in the desert. When he returned home, he found everything broken and torn. Every dish, furniture, and curtain was in pieces and tatters. He thought that his wife was crazy.

He drew two lines in the sand and crossed over them, taking her back to the Land of Djinns. He asked the Sheik to explain the meaning of the two events. The Sheik said that the mother put the child in the fire so that it could become a djinn. He pointed out that there, in the Land of Djinns, was his child, perfect and whole. Next, he explained that when djinns cleaned house, that was the way they did it, by breaking and tearing everything. He pointed at the man's house, in the Land of Djinns, and said, "See, everything is whole."

The man shook his head sadly and left his wife in the Land of Djinns. He crossed the double lines in the sand alone and was back in the world he understood.

JOUHA LOSES HIS DONKEY

Many stories are told of the fool Jouha. A few are given here. Also see the Jouha tales from Kuwait (pp. 33 and 35) and Saudi Arabia (p. 7). Here is a tale shared by Hared Al-Sharji. He heard the story from his grandmother, who lives in the Dhofar Mountains.

When Jouha was traveling in the mountains, he lost his donkey. People told him how sad they were for his loss. But Jouha was relieved. "Thank goodness I only lost my donkey," he told them. "If I had been with it when it got lost, I would be lost too!"

WHO SHOULD RIDE THE DONKEY?

This story was told by the mother of Mohammed Marhoon. Mohammed was a student at the Salalah College of Technology.

Jouha and his son were headed for market, riding on their donkey. As they passed through a village, people began to call out to them.

"Why are you BOTH riding that poor donkey? A donkey like that should only carry one person!"

Jouha was embarrassed. So his son got down and walked along behind the donkey. But in the next village, people were even more adamant.

"Why is a strong man like you riding that donkey, while your son has to walk? You should get down and let HIM ride!"

So Jouha got down, and the son mounted the donkey. But in the next village, people were furious at them for riding the donkey at all.

"That poor donkey cannot carry a load like that. You should not be riding that poor beast!"

Jouha was totally confused. So he told his son to get down, and he and the son hoisted the donkey onto their shoulders and gave IT a ride to market.

When they reached their destination, everyone laughed at them.

"Never mind," said Jouha, as they put the donkey down. "People will never be satisfied."

WHEN JOUHA'S DONKEY PASSES GAS

This tale was told by the father of Reem, a student at Salalah College of Technology.

One day Jouha climbed a tree and started to saw off a limb. Unfortunately, he was sitting on the limb he was sawing off!

A passerby called to him, "Jouha! You are sawing through the branch you are sitting on. You are going to fall when the branch falls!"

Just then the branch was cut through, and sure enough, Jouha fell down with the branch.

Jouha jumped up. "You can tell the future! Tell me something more. Tell me when I am going to die!"

The man protested that he had no idea when Jouha was going to die. But Jouha would not let him go.

"You obviously can tell the future. You just told me I would fall . . . and I did! Please tell me when I am going to die."

So finally the man just made up the first silly thing that came into his head. "Jouha, you will die when your donkey farts."

Jouha went on his way, and after a while, his donkey passed gas. Jouha promptly lay down in the road, thinking he must be dead now.

After a while a group of men came along, arguing about which road to take at the crossroads. One to the right led to one village, the one to the left led to another.

Jouha heard them trying to figure out which road to take to reach the village they wanted. So after a while, he sat up and said, "You take the right road for that village."

The men thanked him and went on. Jouha looked at himself. "That man couldn't predict the future after all," he said. "I'm not even dead!"

THE DJINN OUTSIDE THE WINDOW

This story is about an incident that took place in the Salalah Mountains. It was related by Shaika, a student at Salalah College of Technology. The "Cow Sura" (Surat al-Baqarah) is the longest chapter in the Koran.

A woman lived in the Jebel (Salalah Mountains). One night she was alone in the house. She heard a noise outside the house. So she closed the windows and pulled the curtains. When she went to close one window, she saw a face with long teeth and blood all over it. It was very ugly. The woman was terrified. All night she could hear that djinn outside the house.

In the morning, when other family members came home, she told them what she had seen and what had happened. A Mullah came to read the "Cow Sura" to exorcise the djinn. No one else saw or heard the djinn. But still to this day, she is startled by sounds outside the house. She is still frightened and stays inside her house.

THE SAD STORY OF THE MOTHER CAMEL

Said Al-Mahri, a student at Salalah College of Technology, related this true story.

Saeed had a female camel that was ready to give birth. She did not come to the corral in the evening for several days. When she did return, Saeed went to her.

She led him out into the Jebel and showed him where her baby had been born. She had fought off wild dogs for two days and nights before giving in to exhaustion. She showed Saeed where the dogs had killed and eaten most of her baby camel. He could see the tracks of the struggle and dogs and a few bones left from the baby camel.

His mother camel had tears flowing down from her eyes.

Mother camel photographed in Shisr, Oman by JonLee Joseph.

Here is a traditional story known throughout the Arab world.

The Camel from the Rock

The Koran tells of a time when the prophet Salih was preaching to the people of Thamud. These people had cut homes into the mountainsides and lived well. But they were an arrogant and unkind people. They refused to accept the words of the prophet Salih about the one true God. Instead, they kept worshipping their own idols. Their leader, Jonda, challenged Salih to bring a she-camel big with young out of the solid rock behind them. He swore that if Salih could do this, he and his people would accept the God of Salih.

Salih prayed to God. Then the rocks began to shake and rumble, and out of the rock emerged a large mother camel, big with young. Seeing this, Jonda did believe. But many of the Thamudites still refused to accept God.

Then the she-camel went to the village well and drank up all the water in the well. And after that, she walked through the village giving milk to all who came. Some versions of the story say that the mother camel even cried out, "If anyone wants milk, let him come forth!"

But the Thamudites were not willing to accept the one God. So they cut the hamstrings of the camel and lamed her. And then they proceeded to kill her. But her baby camel was born unharmed and went straight back into the rock from which they had come and disappeared.

Salih warned the Thamudites to stay in their houses for the next three days and repent. He and the believers left the city. Then on the third day, a frightening sound roared down from the heavens, the earth quaked, and the Thamudites, who had not repented, were all killed in their houses.

The rock where the baby camel entered may still be seen. And the town there is now called Mada' in Salih. This is in Saudi Arabia. It is an area of remarkable edifices carved into the cliff sides, somewhat like the Jordanian archeological site of Petra.

Facts: The Remarkable Camel

Camels have a long history in the Middle East. They are believed to have been used by man as early as 3,000 BC. Job, in the Bible, was said to own 6,000 camels.

The desert dweller can drink the camel's milk; eat its meat; use its skin to make water buckets and shields; make rope, clothing, and blankets from its wool; and burn its droppings as fuel.

A camel can carry up to 600 pounds, going 20–30 miles per day, for weeks on end. In a short haul, it can carry up to 1,000 pounds. It can survive on nothing more than thorns, leaves, and bitter desert plants that it encounters on its way.

The camel's sight and smell are very acute. Flaps over the nostrils can be opened to sniff and closed to keep out sand. A double row of eyelashes protects the eyes from blowing sand. Its upper lip is prehensile, allowing it to feel plants before it plucks them to eat. Its broad feet are padded to allow it to move quietly and without pain over sharp flinty ground and to pad with stability in soft sand.

And most remarkable of all, the camel can keep going for three days or more without drinking. If vegetation is available, the camel can live for an even longer time without water, getting moisture from the plants on the ground.

Camel's, however, are said to have very bad tempers. There is a saying, "The camel driver has his plans, but the camel has *his*."

Source: Daniel da Cruz and Paul Lunde, "The Camel in Retrospect," *Saudi Aramco World* (March/ April 1981): 42–48.

WHY LOVE IS BLIND

This folktale was told by Abdulrahman, a student at Salalah College of Technology.

One day, Madness was playing hide-and-seek with Lying-and-Cheating, Love-from-the-Heart, Honor, Duty, and A-Thinking-Mind. Madness hid his eyes and counted to 100. Everything hid. Madness found everything except Love-from-the-Heart. Madness looked and looked. Finally, Lying told Madness where Love-from-the-Heart was hiding. It was inside a flower. So Madness took a stick and poked at the flower, putting its eyes out. That is why today, Love is blind. And from that time, Madness leads Love everywhere.

THE THRIFTY ANT

This story was retold by Sufa, a student at Salalah College of Technology.

Suleiman had the ability to understand and speak with animals. One day, he saw an ant and spoke with it. He asked the ant how much food it ate during a year. The ant replied that it ate three grains of rice in a year.

Then Suleiman put the ant in a box with three grains of rice. After one year, he looked in the box and saw that only one and a half grains of rice had been eaten. He asked the ant why this was.

The ant replied, "When I am outside, God provides. Now that I am in a box, I did not know if you would forget me. I want to live, and so I have eaten less food than I normally would."

THE FAKE BRIDE

A greedy man once had the luck to find the prince passing beneath his house. Quickly he hatched a plan. Mixing his most-expensive perfumes, frankincense, myrrh, sandalwood, and musk, he tossed the beautiful scents out his window so that they perfumed the air all about. He did this just as he spied the prince's entourage coming down the street. So when the prince passed under his window an amazing scent touched his nostrils.

The prince stopped in his tracks. "Whose house is this? Bring the owner out at once!"

When the greedy house owner was brought out, the prince wanted to know where this beautiful scent came from.

"Oh, this is no special scent," lied the greedy man. "This is just the water in which my daughter washed her hands. When she tossed it out into the street, the scent of her hands escaped into the air."

Of course, the prince was fascinated by this story. "If the daughter's hands smell so delicious," he thought, "what must the daughter herself be like?"

So the next day, he sent word that he wished to talk to the man. The prince was so enamored of this mythical girl that he offered a large dowry for her hand in marriage. This is just what the greedy man had hoped for. He agreed at once, and a date was sent for the dowry to arrive and a date for the wedding to take place.

Now, this greedy man did not even *have* a daughter. He planned to take the dowry riches and disappear with them. But to continue the ruse a bit longer, he created a life-sized doll and dressed it in silks and jewels. When the camel procession came to take the bride to the palace for her wedding, the man carried the doll, scarves wrapped around her face for modesty, to the covered stall atop the back of the bride's camel. The man installed the "bride" inside and drew the curtains. Then he bid her good-bye. And taking his falsely gained treasures, he left the country.

As it happened, a genie lived in an upper room along the procession's route. This genie was bothered by a horrid boil on his head, which pained him greatly. When the genie saw the procession passing, he could see from his high window that the "bride" was nothing more than a wooden doll! This tickled him so much that he broke out laughing. And he laughed so hard that the boil broke. Then he laughed even more.

And he had an idea. Calling his own daughter—who was as ugly as all genies are—he worked his genie magic and turned her into a beautiful princess. Then he swished her into the stall on the camel's back where the wooden bride sat and put her in its place.

So it was that the prince was married. And what a wedding night that was!

Trickery, luck, and a happy ending—all from a fling of perfumes.

STRANGERS ON THE ROAD

A man of the Hurth tribe of Oman told this story about the Hinawi and Ghafiri tribes.

A man of the Hinawi tribe was making his way to Muscat when he came upon another traveler. The two men decided to travel together to guard against dangers on the road.

When night came, they made camp, cooked their food, drank their coffee, and laid out their bedding to sleep. But as they chatted, each came to realize that the other was from another tribe.

The man of the Hinawi people was frightened. "This man lying near me is a Ghafiri. What if he decides to murder me during the night?"

And the Ghafiri man was thinking similar thoughts. "This fellow here is a Hinawi. He might try to kill me while I sleep."

Pretending he needed to relieve himself, the Hinawi man went off into the night and loaded his rifle. Soon the Ghafiri man also had to go relieve himself, and he too loaded his rifle.

They lay chatting a while longer and then each pretended to fall asleep. But both men were very alert, thinking, "That stranger might kill me at any moment."

It became very dark, as there was no moon that night. The Hinawi crouched with his gun pointed where he thought the head of the Ghafiri would be, poised to shoot. Sitting like this, he remained awake and alert, ready to fire, all night long. As the first light came, the Hiwawi saw that the Ghafiri was crouched just opposite him, in the same position, with his gun pointing at the head of the Hinawi!

"My friend, why are you pointing your gun at my head this way?" gasped the Hinawi.

"It is just that I had a strange dream," said the Ghafiri. "I dreamed I was out hunting, and I saw a fat gazelle. This gazelle was so fat that I wanted at once to shoot it, so I aimed my gun at the gazelle. And when I awoke, I realized I was aiming my gun at you! But why are you pointing your gun at *me*?"

"I had a similar dream," fabricated the Hinawi man. "But in my dream, there was a huge lion. That lion saw the gazelle in your dream and rushed after it. I followed that bounding lion with my gun, unable to fire, and now I find I am pointing my rifle in the direction in which the lion ran . . . right at your head."

Both men packed their things quickly and continued on their way. And once they reached Muscat, they definitely parted company.

THE JINN BUILDS A ROAD

This tale was collected from Muscat, Oman.

When people used to wonder why there was no road for cars to go to Sur, they were told this story.

Once the people of Sur collected $1,000. They went to an engineer and asked him to build them a road. But the engineer said there was no way. "A road over these hills is impossible to build! You might as well ask the jinn to do it, because man cannot."

So the people of Sur went to the jinn and asked them to build a road. Even the jinn felt it was an impossible task. "There is only one who might be able to do this. His name is Anja. But he will try to trick you. He is known as the prince of cheats. So make sure you have a contract drawn up which is very clear and has witnesses."

So the people went to the wisest man in Sur and had him draw up the contract. It said clearly:

> The road shall run from Muscat to Sur. It shall be 10 yards wide. It shall be completely level so that no part of it shall be up and no part of it shall be down and no part of it shall be above and no part of it below the rest. Its surface will be so smooth that it is like a mirror. And it shall be covered with oil, so there is no dust.

The jinn Anja, looked this over and signed it in front of witnesses. He said, "In seven days, your road will be ready."

When the people of Sur arrived on the seventh day, they did not see a road. There was no wind that day, and the sea lay calm. But where was the road?

"Oh, right here it is," said the jinn.

And he pointed toward the sea. Sure enough, the sea was a level as glass. And on it stretched a broad strip of oil 10 yards wide. And the strip extended all the way across the sea to Muscat.

The people of Sur were furious. They took the jinn to court, and when they went before the Qadhi, the Qadhi examined the contract.

"You did not write anything here about the road being hard and on land," said the Qadhi. "The jinn has met all the stipulations of your contract. You must pay him the $1,000 you promised."

And so the jinn went off laughing with his pay. And the people of Sur remained without a road on land.

TRICKING THE *SAHAR*

The sahar are magical creatures related to the Jinn. They can change shape into a donkey, wolf, bird, and so on. They look like a human but have horns on their heads.

A woman was traveling in Oman when she met an old woman on a mountain road. The old woman asked her to look for a louse in her hair.

"Please look in my hair. A louse is walking there, and I cannot catch him."

So the woman checked the old lady's head for lice and was shocked to see four small horns under the hair. She knew now that the woman was a *sahar*.

The *sahar* said, "Tonight, I am going to Zanzibar. I will return at dawn and will bring you a *nargil*."

The *nargil* is a special kind of coconut which does not grow in Oman. So the woman was amazed the next morning when the *sahar* appeared again on the road before her.

"I was in Zanzibar last night. Here is a *nargil* I brought you."

Now the woman knew for certain that this was a *sahar*, because it was more than 3,000 miles from Oman to Zanzibar.

Thinking quickly, the woman opened her own basket, where she had a flashlight and some chocolate and cookies that she was taking as a present to her relatives in the hills. She said, "You know, while you were in Zanzibar last night, I was in England. Here, I brought you some chocolates from there."

The *sahar* was now convinced that this woman was a *sahar* too, for no ordinary human could go to England and back in one night.

"I didn't realize you were a *sahar* as well," she said. "Then I will leave and do you no harm. Good-bye."

And the *sahar* left her unharmed on the path.

THE BIGGEST LIE

This is a folktale heard in Muscat, Oman.

A fisherman of Muscat once told his friend about the huge fish he had caught.

"It was as big as half my hand!" he said.

"Oh, yes," yawned his friend.

"But before I could take it out of the water, a fish the length of my arm swallowed that fish!"

"Really?"

"And before I could pull *that* fish out . . . a fish as big as an *ox* swallowed them both!"

"Yes, yes . . ."

"And then a fish as big as a truck came up and swallowed them all. . . . And then a fish as big as the mail steamer swallowed that one. . . . And then a fish bigger than all the towns of Muscat, Muttrah, Seeb, and Busher together came and swallowed them all! And this fish was so powerful that it broke my line and escaped with all the other fishes in its mouth."

"Do you know," said his friend, "I went to the bazaar and was amazed at what I saw there. There were 10,000 coppersmiths making an enormous saucepan. It was bigger than all the oil storage tanks of Bahrain. It was so large that it could hold Muscat, Muttrah, Oman, Bahrein, and Karachi all inside!"

The fisherman said, "What a big lie! There never was such a saucepan. You are just making that up."

"Oh, no," replied his friend. "The coppersmiths had heard about the fish you were catching and were making the saucepan to cook the fish that you clumsily let get away."

FOLKTALES FROM QATAR

THE HELPFUL FISH

This is a Cinderella tale from Qatar.

One day, Fsaijrah's stepmother told her, "Take these fish to the seashore and clean them there. Bring them back, and we will cook them for our dinner."

Fsaijrah cut up all of the fish except one small one, but when she lifted her knife to cut that one, it spoke to her.

"Please don't cut me up. Let me go, and I will make you rich."

"Oh, I can't let you go. My stepmother would be angry with me." But she did let the fish slip out of her hands, and it dove into the sea.

When she went back home, her stepmother wanted to see the fish she had cleaned.

"Show me the fish."

"One got away while I was cleaning the others."

So the stepmother made her do without lunch and supper as a punishment.

When the family had finished eating, her stepmother sent her to the sea to throw away the bones. At the seashore, the little fish was waiting for her. He had prepared a beautiful food tray for her, with fish and Qatari clarified butter—the most delicious butter in the world.

A few days later, there was a drums party. The stepmother dressed her own daughter in beautiful clothes and took her to the party. But to Fsaijrah, she said, "There is plenty of work for you here. You stay home."

But as soon as they had gone, the little fish appeared. He brought her a beautiful dress and diamond slippers, and sent her off to the party.

No one recognized the beautifully gowned girl as Fsaijrah, and she hurried home before the others could return. So they had no idea she had been at the drum party.

But she was in such a hurry to reach home that one of her slippers fell off and dropped into a well. She had to return without it.

The next day, the shaikh and his friends passed by the well, and he noticed the glittering shoe. He declared, "Whoever this shoe fits, I will marry."

When the shoe was brought to Fsaijrah's home, the stepmother's daughter tried it on. But the shoe did not fit. But when Fsaijrah put the shoe on, of course it fit perfectly.

So Fsaijrah was engaged to be married to the shaikh.

Her stepmother said, "For her dowry, we want radish, pickled fish, and dates." When they were delivered, the stepmother and her daughter said to Fsaijrah, "Now eat them."

The little fish arrived and dressed her in the most beautiful dress of all, gave her jewelry, and put pearls and red coral on her stomach, which she brought out in the bridal chamber.

As for the daughter of her stepmother, luck was not her ally.

WEALTH, SUCCESS, AND LOVE

Three visitors once arrived at the home of a couple. The wife invited them in for a meal, but they refused to enter unless the entire family was present. So all waited until the son came home. Then the wife once more invited the three to enter and eat.

The visitors refused again. "Only one of us may enter your home," they told her. "You must choose which of us shall come in."

One man stepped forward. "My name is Wealth. Do you wish me to be the one who enters your home?"

A second man stepped forward. "My name is Success. Perhaps you would like me to be the one who enters you home?"

Then the third man stepped forward. "My name is Love."

The three family members had a hard choice to make. They talked it over for some time. The husband wanted to invite Wealth in. The wife preferred to invite Success in. But the son felt that Love should enter. At last the husband and wife agreed that their son's wish should be honored.

"We have decided that Love shall be the one to enter our home," they told the three men.

So Love stepped into the house.

And Wealth and Success followed him in.

"What? We thought only one could enter?" said the couple.

"If you had invited Wealth or Success, we would all have left," they were told.

"But wherever Love goes, Wealth and Success will follow."

ORIGIN OF THE DHOW'S LATEEN SAIL

Small sailing boats in the Arabian Gulf were able to travel widely following the winds. The boats, called "dhow," used a lateen sail, a triangular sail, which was easy to adjust to catch the wind. Pearl fishermen used these dhows to work closer to shore. But many boats traveled to Africa and India.

The village of Al Khor, in northern Qatar, was a center of pearl fishing. The pearl divers worked from small fishing boats which were rowed offshore. But it is said that one day a beautiful woman arrived with her own fleet of dhows. Her fishermen surpassed the local fishermen, and soon she was cutting into their business.

The fishermen of Al Khor challenged this woman to a contest in the hope of getting rid of her. They would have a race with their boats. The one who lost would leave Al Khor and dive for pearls somewhere else. For a while, no one was winning. But suddenly the Al Khor fishermen saw their enemy's boat spring a huge wing! A sail had been raised! Now her boat sped swiftly away, leaving the Al Khor fishermen far behind.

The Al Khor fishermen packed their gear and agreed to move on to another pearl-diving spot. But before they left, the woman offered them a gift. She had her men show them how to construct a sail. Now they too could travel swiftly and improve their catch.

FOLKTALES FROM THE UNITED ARAB EMIRATES

WHY THE HEN CANNOT FLY

There came a time when everything dried up. There was no rain for many days, and the birds were sickening in the heat. So all of the birds met together to decide what to do.

"Let us fly to another place," said the falcon. "We must move on to a land with water to drink."

All of the animals agreed with this. So after some discussion, it was decided that they would fly off the next morning to a more hospitable land.

"Tomorrow," said the falcon, "*Insha'allah*, if Allah wills it, we will fly to another land."

"Tomorrow," said the myna, "*Insha'allah*, we will fly to another land."

"Tomorrow," said the pelican, "*Insha'allah*, we will fly to another land."

And so each bird spoke. And each bird said, "If Allah wills it," as one should always do when one makes plans.

But the hen said, "Tomorrow, I will fly to another land." The other birds all looked at her. But she simply sniffed and refused to add, "*Insha'allah*."

On the following morning, the falcon, the myna, the pelican, the lark, and all the other birds spread their wings and rose up. Off they flew to another land, where there were streams and marshes where they could survive.

But the hen, struggle as she might, found herself unable to fly. And to this day, the hen still finds herself without the gift of flight.

THE SHAIKH'S SHEEP

There was once an old man who had three daughters and one son. Before he died, the father called his son to him.

"I must give you some advice, my son. It is your duty to find husbands for your sisters. But this you must avoid. Do not marry any of your sisters to a stranger.

"And I have more advice for you. Never trust a woman.

"And third, never trust an illegitimate child."

After the father had passed away, some time passed. And then a stranger came to the son and asked for the hand of one of his sisters. The man agreed, even though his father had warned him against this. For a long time, the couple lived happily, so he thought perhaps his father's advice was wrong. He married his other two sisters to cousins, who he knew well.

One day, the man came upon a young child which had been abandoned along the road. He took the child home with him and raised him, even though the child was likely an illegitimate child. The child grew and became dear to him and his mother. When the child reached manhood, he took up work with the shaikh. So this too had turned out well.

The man decided his father's three pieces of advice had been wrong. But he decided to test one of the pieces of advice: never tell a secret to a woman.

The man found a sheep which belonged to the shaikh. He took it and hid it away, looking after it very well. Then he went to the butcher and bought meat and fat and got some sheep's wool. Taking these things home, he gave them to his wife.

"Where did you get these things?" his wife wanted to know.

"Oh, I cannot tell you," he said. "That is something that must be kept a secret."

His wife pestered him with questions, until at last he said, "Well, I will tell you the secret. But you must promise not to tell another person about this." And he told her that he had stolen the shaikh's sheep and slaughtered it.

Now the shaikh soon missed his sheep and sent servants everywhere to search for it. When it could not be found, an old woman came to the shaikh and promised that she could discover who had stolen his sheep.

The old woman went from house to house, showing a finger wrapped in a bloody cloth and saying she had cut her finger. She needed fat to cure the wound. No one had any fat to give her. But when she came to the home of the man who had hidden the sheep, his wife brought out fat for her.

"This is just what I needed!" said the old woman. "But where did you get this fat?"

"Oh, that is a secret," said the man's wife.

But the old woman begged her to tell, and soon enough she spilled it all out.

"But you must promise not to tell anyone," said the wife.

Of course, the old woman went right to the shaikh.

"Bring that man to me at once," demanded the shaikh.

The young boy the man had raised was working for the shaikh, so he said, "No problem. I will go and arrest him." And thus the illegitimate boy was the one who went to arrest the man who had raised him.

"We cannot allow thievery in our land," said the shaikh. "As a fine, I require you to bring me 10 camels."

The man went right away to ask help of his brothers-in-law. The brother-in-law who was a stranger gave him one sickly camel. "That's all I can spare," he told him. When the man went to his other two brothers-in-law, those who were cousins, they hurried to bring him the camels he needed.

Then the man went and brought the shaikh's sheep from where he had hidden it and took the sheep to the shaikh. He explained how he had hidden the sheep and told the "secret" to his wife to test the wisdom of his father's three pieces of advice.

"And I see that all three were good pieces of advice," he told the shaikh. "For the illegitimate child treated me cruelly, even though I had raised him. And my brother-in-law who was a stranger refused to give me much help, while my brothers-in-law who were relatives aided me in every way possible."

Then the man loaded the camels of his helpful brothers-in-law with rice and flour and dates and took them back to them. But the sickly camel of the third brother-in-law he returned, with the advice to look after his animals better.

And thus it was proved that following the advice of one's elders is wise indeed.

THE FISHERMAN'S DAUGHTER

There once was a fisherman's daughter who was being looked after by a cruel stepmother who had two daughters of her own. Of course, those daughters got all the good food and nicest clothes and did no work at all. The fisherman's daughter had to do all the work for the household and was dressed only in the oldest of rags.

One day, the stepmother sent the girl to clean five fish. She took them down to the seashore and was cutting the fish up, when the last fish, which was still alive, started trembling and begged the girl, "Please don't cut me up. Put me back in the water so that I may live. If you do that, I will come to help you when you need me. Just look for me here beside this rock."

So the girl felt pity on the fish and tossed it back into the sea.

But when she reached home, her stepmother was furious. "I sent you to clean FIVE fish. You return with only FOUR. No supper for YOU tonight."

The girl went back down to the sea, weeping, and sat beside the rock where she had tossed back the fish. Soon the fish itself came up. When he heard of her troubles, he brought up to her the most delicious foods imaginable, and she ate until she was full.

A few weeks later there was to be a wedding at the shaikh's palace. Everyone was invited to attend the celebration. Of course, the fisherman's daughter had to stay home and clean and cook and was not allowed to go to the wedding. But when she told her friend the fish about this, he came up with all sorts of beautiful clothes and jewels, and even a pair of golden slippers. And the fish gave her a piece of advice.

"When you enter the palace, be sure to pass by the *barza* where the shaikh's son is resting. I would like for him to lay eyes on you."

This is exactly what she did, and when the shaikh's son saw her, he fell in love immediately. The shaikh's son hurried out and followed the girl. But seeing herself pursued, she ran off home. However, her golden slippers dropped off just as she passed the water trough where the shaikh's horses watered. When the shaikh's son came back, after giving up on chasing her, he found those golden slippers.

The next day, the shaikh sent his servants to visit all the homes in the area where daughters could be found. They tried the slippers on every girl, but none of them were a fit. When they came to the fisherman's house, the stepmother hid the girl in a *tannur* and had her own daughters brought out to try on the slippers. Of course, they did not fit.

"Is there no other girl in this house?" asked the shaikh's men.

"None at all," lied the stepmother.

But just then the cock started crowing, "My ugly aunts are on the bed, and my beautiful aunt is in the oven!" The cock just kept on crowing this and would not stop.

So the shaikh's men searched the entire house, and there in the oven, they found the beautiful fisherman's daughter. The slippers fit her perfectly.

So the fisherman's daughter was taken to the shaikh's son, and he was so happy that he married her immediately. And they lived in much happiness.

FOLKTALES FROM YEMEN

THE QUEEN OF SHEBA VISITS KING SOLOMON

The Queen of Sheba is believed to be Queen Bilquis of Saba. The country of Saba included the present-day country of Yemen. Here is a brief account of Sheba's visit. You can read more details in the Old Testament, First Book of Kings, chapter 10.

When the Queen of Sheba heard about the fame of Solomon, who was king of Israel, she traveled to Jerusalem to pose some hard questions to him about his faith. She brought a camel train with many spices and gold and precious stones.

They talked together, and Solomon answered all of her questions. The queen was impressed by Solomon's wisdom.

"It was a true report that I heard in my own land about your acts and your wisdom," she told him. "I couldn't believe it until I had seen it with my own eyes. But in fact, your wisdom even exceeds what I was told. Your people and your servants are truly lucky to stand before you and hear your wisdom." And she called blessings on God, who had put Solomon on the throne.

Then King Solomon gave her anything she asked for and more, and she returned home with her servants with many presents.

QUEEN BILQUIS VISITS KING SUYLEIMAN

The Koran gives other details and a more elaborate story (Koran, sura 27).

It happened that a hoopoe bird came to King Suyleiman one day. The bird brought news of a land far to the south called Saba, where a beautiful queen ruled. But the bird told Suyleiman that the people of that land worshipped the sun. They did not know about the one true god, Allah.

So Suyleiman sent the queen, whose name was Bilquis, a letter asking her to change her religion and accept the one true God. She wasn't sure what to do. Her counselors reminded her that they were very tough and could go to war against this Suyleiman if she wished. But the queen was afraid of what might happen should they lose a war to Suyleiman. So she decided to go and visit him.

Suyleiman was delighted that she was coming. He wanted her throne to be brought to his palace so that she could be seated on her own throne when she arrived. One of the jinn under his control offered to bring it, but he couldn't bring it quick enough for Suyleiman. Then one of the jinn who had converted said that he could do it immediately. And the throne appeared in Suyleiman's palace.

Suyleiman had ordered a crystal palace built to receive the queen, and when she entered, she was amazed to see her throne waiting for her there.

In some versions of the story, the queen sets riddles to Suyleiman. It is told that before going to visit him she first sent a present of an unpierced pearl and a pierced emerald. She asked that he pierce the pearl and thread the emerald. Suyleiman called a wood carver, who pierced the pearl. But he was stymied by how to pass a thread through the tiny winding hole in the emerald. Then he heard a tiny voice down by his feet.

"I can do it, O prophet of the Lord." It was a tiny worm.

The worm took the thread in its mouth and entered the hole in the emerald. In a few moments it emerged from the other side, dragging the thread behind. So King Suyleiman put the pearl and the emerald back in the bottle they had been sent in and returned them to the queen. When she saw this, she prepared to visit him.

On arriving, the queen tested Suleyiman with another riddle. "What water belongs to neither heaven nor earth?"

Suleyiman came up with a good answer for that one. "When my horses gallop, the sweat runs off of them. If I collect this water, it is from neither heaven nor earth."

THE MIGHTY DYKE OF MA-RIB

The dike at Ma-rib was about 1,800 feet long (550 m) and irrigated over 4,000 acres of land. It was built by the Sabbaen people (950–115 BC).

One night, Queen Zarifa heard a voice in the night.

"Zarifa, you may choose. You may have a child to bring you delight or knowledge to fill your soul. Which do you choose?"

Without hesitation, Zarifa spoke. "I choose knowledge."

At once she felt a hand placed on her head. And she realized that knowledge was entering her being. And then she felt a hand placed on her womb, and she knew she would be barren from that moment.

The king and queen lived happily, until one night the queen had a horrid dream. "I saw thunderbolts shattering our world!" she told the king when she awoke. But he told her it was nothing more than a bad dream.

Some days later, the king went down to the orchard with two slave girls. Zarifa walked down with one of her slave boys to find him. Suddenly, on the path, she saw three rats standing up on their hind legs with their paws over their eyes. Zarifa knew this was a bad omen. She crouched down and covered her own eyes.

"Tell me when the rats are gone," she directed her slave boy. Then she continued on.

Suddenly, a tortoise leaped out of the stream and landed on its back. This too must be an evil omen.

When she reached the orchard, the trees were swaying, though there was no breeze. She told her husband of these omens. And falling into a trance she began to forecast the destruction of their valley.

"The Dike of Ma'rib will fall!" she wailed. "Our land will be destroyed!"

The king did not want to believe this horrible fate. She told him to go to the dam and watch. If he saw rats burrowing among the rocks there, he must know it was true. Sure enough, the rats were scurrying about and digging right into the face of the dam; boulders were starting to roll away.

King 'Amr took all of his people, and they fled their valley. He led his own and many other tribes away from the disaster that would soon befall. Because of Queen Zarifa, the people were saved. And the dam did break.

THE YEAR OF THE WHITE ELEPHANT

The event described in this story is important in Islamic tradition as this is believed to have occurred in the year that Prophet Mohammad was born.

An Abyssinian ruler, named Abraha, once crossed over from Ethiopia and took control of the area of Yemen. Wishing to compete with the strong religion centered on the Ka'ba in Mecca, he had a great Christian temple, called Al-Qalis, built in San'a, the capital of Yemen. This failed to attract the attention he had hoped, though. So he mounted a great army and went to Mecca to destroy the Ka'ba so that people would make their pilgrimage to his temple instead.

As Abraha neared Mecca, his army captured all of the camels and sheep that belonged to the people of Mecca. He had captured over 200 camels which belonged to Abd Al-Muttalib, the chief of the Quraysh tribe, who were the custodians of the Ka'ba. Abraha then sent a message to Abd Al-Mutalib saying that he came to destroy the Ka'ba, not to conquer the people.

Abd al-Muttalib went to Abraha's tent and asked to speak to him. Abraha thought Abd al-Muttalib had come to beg him to not touch the Ka'ba. But Abd al-Muttalib simply asked for his camels to be returned.

Abraha sneered at him. "I thought you were a man of sincerity who would come to beg that I not destroy your sacred site. Instead, you just ask for livestock."

But Abd al-Muttalib said simply, "I am the master of the camels. I must defend them. Our Sacred House belongs to the Lord. He will defend it."

So Abraha returned the camels. But he also prepared to take over Mecca city and the Ka'ba. He was surprised to see that no people tried to defend the sacred site.

Abraha had brought with him one extraordinarily large and impressive elephant imported from Africa, a white elephant named Mahmud. He assumed that this beast would terrorize the people of Mecca. But when he approached the Ka'ba with the beast, the huge elephant knelt to the Ka'ba and then turned and walked away. Abraha goaded the elephant back to the Ka'ba. But once again, it bowed to the Ka'ba and then turned and walked away. No matter how he tried, Abraha could not get the beast to attack the sacred site.

Then suddenly the air was filled with fantastical green birds. Each bird carried a stone in its beak and stones in each claw. The birds swooped in and began to drop the stones on the army of Abraha. Each soldier hit by a stone was poisoned and fell dead, until the field was littered with dead bodies like bent straw. Abraha's forces were defeated, and the people of Mecca returned safely to their homes.

THE MANLY MAIDEN

Here is a Yemeni version of a story found in The Arabian Nights. You will notice the device of a frame story and other stories within the story. This is common in many of the Arabian Nights tales.

THE GIFT OF A BIRD

A merchant who was leaving for a trip wanted to give his wife something to comfort her while he was gone. In the marketplace, he met a vendor who offered him a little goldfinch for sale.

"This bird sells for a thousand dinars," said the vendor. "Who buys it shall not regret it. And who buys it shall regret it."

The merchant was befuddled by this statement. What could it mean?

"Just buy the bird and you will find out," replied the vendor. "But you must know that this little bird eats only almonds and raisins and drinks only milk and honey."

The merchant carried the goldfinch home to his wife. "Take good care of this bird while I am gone," he told her. "It will keep you good company. But be sure to feed it almonds and raisins each day and give it milk and honey to drink. Care for it well until I return." And the merchant set off on his journey.

The wife leaned out her upper window to watch him go, and just at that moment, the sultan's son was passing by. When he saw her unveiled beauty leaning out of the window, he fell instantly in love. He returned home and took to bed ill with longing for her.

The sultan could not find out what was causing his son such sickness. He sent for doctors, but none of them could find a cause. So he sent for a wise old woman, and she soon discovered the problem.

"I will bring the woman you love to your side," she promised. And they made a plan.

The next day, the old woman came to the house of the merchant's wife. She knocked on the door and called, "Would you come with me, my dear? My daughter is to be married, and we need you to attend the wedding."

The merchant's wife replied, "I am sorry, but I will not leave the house until my husband has returned safely from his journey."

But the old woman pleaded and begged and said her daughter would not consent to be married unless the merchant's wife attended.

So at last the merchant's wife dressed herself; made up her eyes with kohl; painted her hands, arms, and feet; and was leaving the house to go.

As she went down the first step of the house, she turned back to the goldfinch. "Dear little bird, good-bye."

But the goldfinch answered, "My lady, have you completely forgotten me?"

"Why do you say that, dear goldfinch?"

"Just wait a moment and I will tell you a story. Will you be patient and listen to my tale?"

"With pleasure, dear goldfinch," said the lady. So the bird began at once.

THE GOLDFINCH'S FIRST TALE

There once was a boy and girl who were cousins. They were madly in love, but their fathers were mortal enemies. The two decided to elope on a ship and be married far from their families.

On the day the ship was to sail, the two went on board, but the girl realized that they had no provisions for the journey. So she sent her cousin onshore to buy things in the marketplace. She urged him to hurry, for the ship was due to sail soon.

But the boy began to look at this and that in the marketplace and lost track of time. Meanwhile, the girl had sunk down on a sail on the ship and fell asleep. When she awoke, the ship had sailed, and her cousin was not on board.

The ship's captain found her crying. And when he had heard her story, he took her into his own cabin. And soon he decided that he would marry her himself.

The girl had no idea how to escape this, so she pretended to go along with him. She spent much time watching how he steered the ship and managed things. And one day, when the ship moored at an island so the passengers could stroll on the shore and picnic, the girl brewed coffee for the captain and slipped opium in the cup. As soon as he was asleep, she called everyone back on board the ship. Then she went down into the stokehold, got up the steam, cranked the engine, and gave orders to the Somali crew to set off.

When the ship's captain woke up, he found himself alone on a desert island. Then he did repent having bothered the girl.

"Lady," said the goldfinch, "if you go to this wedding, you shall repent of it, just as that captain repented."

"You are quite right," said the merchant's wife. And she made an excuse to the old woman and refused to go.

But the next day, here came the old woman again with another reason why the merchant's wife just had to get dressed and come out with her. After many refusals, the merchant's wife finally did dress, make up her eyes, anoint her body, and start to leave the house.

"Dear little bird, good-bye," she said, as she passed the goldfinch in its cage.

"Good luck, my lady. Have you forgotten me?"

"What do you lack, dear bird?"

"Do you know what happened to the girl?" asked the bird.

"No," said the women.

"Then wait a little and I will tell you."

THE BIRD'S SECOND STORY

After the girl had taken her passengers to their destinations, she anchored her steamer in the harbor and went ashore to see the town. As she was passing through the market, she met Shachbender, the merchant prince. He invited her to his huge house and asked about her business. She told him the whole story of her cousin and the ship's captain.

"What has happened, has happened," said Shachbender, the merchant prince. "Since the Fates have brought you to our city, it has doubtless been decided by them that you should become my wife."

The girl had to find out a way to escape this. She told Shachbender that she would marry him only if he would find 40 couples to wed at the same time. Soon he had lined up the 40 couples to be married. But the girl talked secretly to all of the brides and convinced them to run away with her to see the wide world.

So on the day when the weddings were to take place, Shachbender and the 40 grooms and the 40 brides all came on board the girl's ship for the wedding. She served the men coffee . . . with opium. And soon they were all snoring soundly.

Then she had her sailors haul the sleeping men ashore. She went down in the stokehold, got up the steam, cranked the engine, and she and the 40 brides set off for adventures.

After a few days, they came to a green island and all went ashore to drink fresh springwater and relax among the trees. But as soon as they were taking their ease, out jumped forty-one robbers and grabbed them.

"Allah has delivered you to us!" cried the robbers. "You are ours!"

Thinking quickly, the girl welcomed the robbers. "We desire nothing but to be agreeable to you. Do come on board our vessel and we will prepare food and drink for you all."

So the robbers came on board, laughed, and relaxed, and drank coffee . . . laced with opium.

Then she had her Somali crewmen haul the robbers ashore, and she and her friends stripped the clothing from the sleeping robbers and stuck radishes on their bums to insult them. Then she and the girls all put on the robber's clothing and returned to their ship.

When the robbers woke up the next morning, they repented very much of having gotten involved with these ladies.

Then the goldfinch spoke directly to the merchant's wife. "You, too, will repent, dear lady, if you go out with this old woman."

"You are correct," said the merchant's wife. And making excuses, she went back into the house.

Of course, on the next day, the old woman was back, begging the merchant's wife to come with her for some important reason. All of this was of course a ruse, as she really just wanted to lead the merchant's wife to the house of the sultan.

Once more the merchant's wife prepared herself, put on her jewelry, and descended the stairs. And once more she bid the goldfinch good-bye.

"You have certainly forgotten me, dear lady," said the goldfinch.

"Why must you always say that? Can't I just go to the wedding with this old woman?"

"Do you know what happened next to the girl?"

"No, I don't."

"Well, wait a little while and I will tell you."

Well, the merchant's wife was quite exasperated by the goldfinch always stopping her. But she really did want to know what happened to the girl. So she sat down to listen.

THE GOLDFINCH'S THIRD TALE

After the girl and her companions had dressed themselves as men, they sailed away into the wide world until they came to a great port. There they went ashore and came near the palace. As they approached the palace, they entered a huge crowd of people and asked what was going on.

"The king has died and left no children," they were told. "It is our custom in such a case for the queen to go up on the roof of the palace and throw the crown down onto the crowd. The man on whose head the crown falls becomes the next king."

Just as they heard these words, the girl felt a hard *thunk* strike her head. She put up her hand . . . and there was the crown . . . stuck right on top of her head!

"God bless our king!" called all of the people, and she was hauled up to the palace and set upon the throne. She was now the new sultan of the country! And of course, because of her clothing, everyone believed that she was a man.

She should have married the queen by rights, but the viziers thought a beardless boy was not proper for the spouse of an older queen. So instead she was betrothed to be wed to the beautiful daughter of the grand vizier.

Of course, this presented problems. On the wedding night, the sultan (our girl) just chatted and joked with the bride all night long. But after a few nights of this, she finally had to admit the truth and reveal that she was not a man, but a woman herself. By this time though, the vizier's daughter had come to care for the sultan (our girl), and she agreed to keep the secret. Even the grand vizier agreed to keep this quiet to avoid disgrace.

Then the girl had a plaster mold of her face made and set up in markets all around the country. Soon, sure enough, her long-lost love, her cousin, came upon one of these statues. He made such a row when he saw it that he was hauled to the palace and taken before the sultan. She did not reveal her true identity to him but had him escorted to a beautiful roof arbor to wait.

The next day, along came Shachbender, and he spied one of the statues. He too raised a fuss at the sight and was hauled before the sultan. She had him also put into a room to wait.

Then she went to the grand vizier's daughter. "I might have found a suitable husband for you," she said. "Shachbender is a very wealthy man and a good man. He was just not the right man for me."

"I won't marry Shachbender, or anyone else, until you have found your own true love," said the grand vizier's daughter. "My life is now bound to yours."

Then she called the 40 maidens and told them that Shachbender had arrived in court.

"Now you can all go back and marry the 40 grooms you left behind," she said.

But they swore that they would never leave her side, but they would marry the grooms if they came to this country.

So the sultan (our maid) called Shachbender and revealed to him everything. She swore him to secrecy and then sent him back to fetch the 40 grooms. And he returned with the 40 grooms and their fathers and mothers and aunts and uncles and cousins for the wedding ceremonies.

And when all this was arranged, she went up to the arbor on the roof and revealed herself to her long-lost cousin love. At first, he would not believe that it was she. But when she threw off her headdress and her robes, he could not believe his eyes. Then they sat in the arbor, and she told him everything that had happened since the hour of their parting.

"And you have lost one love, but have gained two," she said. And she told him of the grand vizier's daughter, to whom she was married.

So they went to the councilors and told them everything. It was decided, "Since he is your cousin, he shall be the sultan and you shall be the queen, and you shall rule together."

So they were married. And afterward, he also married the daughter of the grand vizier, and they all had children and grandchildren and lived happily ever after.

When the merchant's wife heard that the story was finished, she got up to go with the old woman, but just then the merchant himself returned. He knew at once that something was amiss and questioned the old woman until he got her to admit that she was really just trying to take his wife to the sultan's son. So the sultan's son did not get to meet with the merchant's wife after all, and they say he died of love.

When the merchant heard of how the goldfinch had saved his wife three times by his long tales, the merchant took the little bird in his hands and stroked it. "Now I know what the vendor told me, 'Who does not buy this bird shall regret it.' But can you explain to me why he also said, 'Who buys this bird for one thousand dinars shall repent of it?'"

"Oh, that I can gladly do," said the goldfinch. "Only open your hand and you shall see at once."

So the merchant opened his hand . . . and the goldfinch unfolded his wings and rose into the air and disappeared.

That happened to them, but this happened to us.
On their roof is sheep dung, on ours, almonds and raisins.
If we have spoken the truth, it is God's truth; if we have lied, God forgive us.
Go home quickly, or the dog will eat up your supper.
And forgive us for wearying you. We in turn forgive you for being such a nuisance to us.

ARABIC PROVERBS AND PROVERB TALES

ARABIC PROVERBS

The proverb has a long history of usage in the Arab world. In 1107, a collection of 3,461 Arabic proverbs was completed by Abu al-Qasim az-Zamakhshari. Even earlier, Ahmad ibn Muhammad al-Maidani completed a book of 4,766 proverbs, which was based on 50 earlier books of proverbs. The Koran and the Hadith are rich sources of proverbs. And Arabic poetry and literature are sources of even more proverbs.

Here are a few Arabic proverbs:

Man can have nothing but what he strives for.
—Koran, an-Naim 39

Learning is a treasury whose keys are queries.
—Conversations, Abu Nairn

The remedy of time is patience.
—Conversations, Abu Daud and at-Tirmizi

In seeking honey, expect the sting of bees.
—Al-Mutanabbi

Ride the tributaries to reach the sea.
—Al-Mutanabbi

Repetitive visits cause boredom.

One hand does not clap.

A seeker of knowledge and a seeker of money never meet.

PROVERBS FROM THE UNITED ARAB EMIRATES

An eye is not above the eyebrow.

In what way will barking dogs affect the clouds.

Hair falling from the moustache rests on the beard.
(Any action by your relatives affects you, and any of your actions affect your relatives.)

An eye is tempted by what is concealed, and does not desire what is exposed openly.
(This is quoted to young women.)

HUNAIN'S SLIPPERS

Here is a folktale from which a proverb springs. The story is the origin of the Arabic saying, "He returned with Hunain's slippers." If someone comes back without achieving their aims, this might be said.

There once was a cobbler named Hunain. One day, a stingy Bedouin came to his shop and bargained for a pair of slippers. But the man refused to pay a proper price. He bargained all day long for these slippers and then just went off without buying them. Hunain was infuriated that the man had wasted his time like that. So he made a plan to get back at him.

Hunain rode out on the road where he knew the Bedouin would be passing. There he dropped one of the slippers the man had been bargaining for. Then he went a bit farther down the road and dropped the second slipper.

When the Bedouin came on the first slipper, he thought, "That's a slipper just like the one I bargained for with Hunain. Well, one slipper is no use by itself." So he went on his way.

But soon he discovered the *second* slipper. "Here is the mate to that slipper I just saw!" So he jumped off his camel and hurried back to pick up the first slipper.

As soon as the Bedouin was out of sight, Hunain came out from where he had been hiding and made off with the Bedouin's camel and gear. Thus, the Bedouin returned to his tribe with nothing but the pair of Hunain's slippers.

A CRAB HAS DROWNED A CAMEL

This Omani tale gives the origin of another proverb. When a small misfortune leads to something terrible, people say, "A crab has drowned a camel."

A man coming to Muscat leading his camel stopped to eat some dates. He lay down to sleep beneath a tree beside the sea. As he slept, the rope of his camel slipped from his hand.

Just then a crab came up from the sea and discovered the rope. It was still scented with dates from the man's hands, so the crab picked up the end of the rope and carried it back to the sea with it, walking sidewise down the beach as crabs do. The camel felt a slight tug on its rope, so it got up and followed where the rope led. The crab hauled the rope right into the sea. And the camel followed along. There the poor camel floundered about and was drowned.

When the man woke up, he found his dead camel floating by the beach. He couldn't understand why his camel would have gone into the sea. But then he saw the tracks of the crab leading from where he slept down into the water and the tracks where the rope had been dragged. Now he understood how a small thing had caused this great misfortune.

RIDDLES

RIDDLES FROM THE UNITED ARAB EMIRATES

A blue bowl in an empty river, at night it is filled.

Answer: The sky

Whenever it increases, it decreases.

Answer: The moon

What piece of land has the sun shone on only once?

Answer: The bottom of the Red Sea where Moses parted it.

What eats and is never sated, but when it drinks it dies?

Answer: Fire

What lengthens and shortens at the same time?

Answer: Your life

It overpowers my father and yours. It overpowers the sultan and the king.

Answer: Sleep

It sticks like glue and to everything it sticks.

Answer: A name

Doors which are open during the day and closed at night. When you look into them, you see yourself.

Answer: Your eyes

We watch it, but it doesn't watch us. We hear it, but it doesn't hear us.

Answer: The television

The brother of a child's mother is his maternal uncle. This is an important person in the child's life. Two riddles play on this.

Your paternal aunt is your father's sister. Who is her son's maternal uncle to you?

Answer: Your father

Mother of your brother and sister to your maternal uncle, wife of your father. Who is she to you?

Answer: Your mother

More Arab riddles:

Its shadow is inside its stomach.

Answer: The well

It is white inside and black outside.

Answer: A cauldron

ARABIC WORDS

Many of the words we use in the English language have origins in the Arabic language. Here are just a few.

Alchemy (from al-kimya): to change a metal into another metal
Alcohol (from al-khol, al-khul): the black eye powder used by women, and thus a pure substance
Alcove (from al-qubbah): the arch
Algebra (from al-jabr): reunion of broken parts
Algorithm (from Al-Khwarizmi): the inventor of the concept
Alkali (from al-qili): ashes of the saltwort plant
Almanac (from al-manakh): almanac
Average (from awariya): damaged goods
Carafe (from gharrafah): a bottle
Cipher (from sifr): zero or empty
Garbled (from gharbala): sift or select
Ghoul (from al-ghul): demon
Jar (from jarrah): an earthen water vessel
Racket, as in tennis racket (from raha): the palm of the hand
Sofa (from suffah): a long bench

STARS WITH ARABIC NAMES

Aldebaran, Algol, Altair, Betelgeuse, Rigel, and Vega

FOOD WORDS

Coffee (from qahwah gahwah)
Julep, Marzipan, Sherbet, Sugar, and Syrup
Lemon (from Arabic laymun)
Mocha (from the Yemeni port city)
Spices: Caraway, Cumin, and Saffron

FABRICS

Damask (from Damascus)
Muslin (from Mosul, Iraq)
Sash (from shash): muslin
Sequin (from sikkah): a die for striking coins
Tabby (from al-Tabbiya, area of Baghdad): striped silk pattern or striped cat

COLORS

Azure, Carmine, Crimson, and Lilac

SEAFARING WORDS

Admiral (from amir-al): a shortened form of amir-al-bahr, prince of the sea
Arsenal (from dar as-sina'ah): workshop
Mizzen (from mazzan): mast

OTHER ARABIC WORDS

Adobe, Bedouin, Caliper, Caliph, Camphor, Crocus, Elixir, Genie, Minaret, Mosque, Nadir, Sheik, Sultan, Talisman, and Zenith

TALE NOTES

MOTIF AND TYPE SOURCES

Aarne, Antti, and Stith Thompson. *The Types of the Folktale*. Helsinki: Suomalainen Tiedeakatemia, 1973.

El-Shamy, Hasan M. *Folk Traditions of the Arab World: A Guide to Motif Classification*. Bloomington: Indiana University Press, 1995.

MacDonald, Margaret Read. *The Storyteller's Sourcebook: A Subject, Title, and Motif Index to Folklore Collections for Children*. 1st edition. Detroit: Gale Research, 1982.

MacDonald, Margaret Read, and Brian W. Sturm. *The Storyteller's Sourcebook: A Subject, Title, and Motif Index to Folklore Collections for Children: 1983–1999*. Detroit: Gale Research, 2000.

Thompson, Stith. *Motif-Index of Folk-Literature*. Bloomington: Indiana University Press, 1966.

LUQMAN THE WISE

Information about Luqman is taken from "Aesop of the Arabs" by Paul Lunde, *Saudi Aramco World* (March/April 1974), 2–3, and "Lukman and the Seven Falcons," in *Fabled Cities, Princes & Jinn from Arab Myths and Legends* by Khairat Al-Saleh (New York: Schocken, 1985), 40–42. A useful article on Luqman is found on *Wikipedia*: http://en.wikipedia.org/wiki/Luqman. The Koran, sura 31, reveals some of Luqman's advice.

Motif: El-Shamy J191.3 Luqman as wise man. El-Shamy cites seven Arabic sources, including Palestinian.

THE DOVE, THE PARTRIDGE, AND THE CROW

This tale is retold by Nadia Jameel Taibah.

Motifs A2411.2.1.6 Color of crow; A2375.2 Nature of animal's feet; A2332.5 Color of animal's eyes; Q263 Lying punished.

THE LION, THE WOLF, AND THE FOX

This is an Aesop fable. A Russian version adds the "learned to divide from the wolf" motif.

Type 51 The Lion's Share cites versions that are Greek, Argentinian, African American, African, Slovenian, Flemish, and French.

Motif J811.1 The Lion's Share. Ass divides booty equally between himself, fox, and lion. Lion eats ass. Fox then divides: gives lion meat and he takes bones.

THE ANT AND THE LOUSE

This tale is a tradition from Nadia Jameel Taibah's family.

Motif Z49.13 Chain of killings: bulbul destroys flower and is killed by cat, etc.

SIGNS

This tale is a tradition from Nadia Jameel Taibah's family. MacDonald cites sources from Iran, Georgia (Caucasus), and Ireland. MacDonald and Sturm cite sources from England and Japan.

Type 924 Discussion by Sign Language cites variants from Czechoslovakia, Lithuania, Scotland, Sweden, Italy, Argentina, Brazil, India, China, and Turkey, among others.

Motif H607.1.1 Discussion by symbols. Sign language.

JOUHA AND HIS DONKEYS

Nadia Jameel Taibah heard this tale from her aunt Salha. *The Storyteller's Sourcebook* cites versions from Syria, Armenia, Turkey, and North Africa. Anntti Aarne's Type Index cites variants from Finland, Estonia, Sweden, Iceland, France, Spain, the Netherlands, Italy, Hungary, Slovenia, Serbia, Russia, Greece, China, Turkey, and England. Also see the picture book *How Many Donkeys?: An Arabic Counting Tale*, retold by Margaret Read MacDonald and Nadia Jameel Taibah. Illus. Carol Liddiment (Chicago: Albert Whitman, 2009).

Type 1288A Numbskull cannot find ass he is sitting on.

Motifs J2022 Numbskull cannot find ass he is sitting on; J2031 Counting wrong by not counting oneself.

THE POOR LADY'S PLAN

This tale is a tradition from Nadia Jameel Taibah's family.

Motifs: N611.4 Thief hears owner of house singing and thinks himself detected; N612 Numbskull talks to himself and frightens the robbers away.

THROW YOUR PUMPKIN AND PICK ME UP

This tale is a tradition from Nadia Jameel Taibah's family.

Motif Q2 Kind and Unkind. Churlish person disregards requests of old person and is punished. Courteous person complies and is rewarded.

THE ANNOYING DOVE

This tale is a tradition from Nadia Jameel Taibah's family. MacDonald's *Storyteller's Sourcebook* cites variants from India, Pakistan, Uganda, Thailand, the United States, and Spain.

Motif Z49.3 The bird indifferent to pain. A man catches a mango-bird . . . cooks it, eats it, the bird flies out of his nose.

THE SEVEN BUCKTHORN PICKERS

This tale is a tradition from Nadia Jameel Taibah's family.

Motifs: G512.3 Ogre burned in his own oven; G526 Ogre deceived by feigned ignorance of hero. Hero must be shown how to get into oven (or the like).

A WISE YOUNG BOY

This tale is told of the Islamic legal scholar Abu Hanifah (699–767).

Motifs: H659.1.1 What is oldest? God; H561.4 King and clever youth. King asks questions: youth returns riddling answers. Type 921.The King and the Peasant's Son.

THE KING, THE PRINCE, AND THE NAUGHTY SHEEP

A preschool version of this story was created by Nadia Taibah. The Koran (sura 21:76) refers to this event.

THE MIRACLE OF THE SPIDER'S WEB

This legend is known throughout the Islamic world. It also appears in the lore of several other cultures. Stith-Thompson cites variants of this motif from Turkey, Lapland, India, Japan, and Africa's Fang people and in Jewish tradition. El-Shamy cites an Egyptian variant. MacDonald cites Indonesian and Jewish variants. MacDonald and Sturm cite an Arabian version and a variant in which the spider hides Mary and Joseph and the baby Jesus.

Type 967 The Man Saved by a Spider Web includes variants from Catalonia, England, the Netherlands, and the United States.

Motif B523.1 Spider-web over hole saves fugitive.

'UMAR IBN AL-KHATTAB COOKS FOOD FOR HUNGRY CHILDREN

In the legend of the second Caliph, 'Umar Ibn Al-Khattab, he is known for his charitable acts. He established a welfare system for the poor, orphans, widows, elderly, and disabled.

MAKKI AND KAKKI

This is a variant of *Motif Q2. Kind and Unkind.* Also motifs *J2400 Foolish imitation*; and *J2415 Foolish imitation of lucky man. Because one man has good luck, a numskull imitates and thinks he will have equal luck. He is disappointed.* Tales on this theme are popular throughout the world. Hassan El-Shamy cites *Motif J2415* Tales from Yemen and Kuwait. Stith Thompson gives variants from India, China, the West Indies, Italy, England, and more and in Arab tradition. "Makki and Kakki" includes *Motifs D1026 Magic dung of animal* and *B103.1 Treasure dropping animal.* Hassan El-Shamy cites tales from Iraq (gold-dropping ass), along with Egypt and Sudan (gold-dropping cat). A Saudi version appears as "Makki's Mother," in *Folktales from Saudi Arabia* by Lamya' Muhammad Salih Ba-ashin (Jiddah: Lamia Baeshen, 2002), 31–35.

THE MOUSE AND THE EGGSHELL BOAT

This tale is similar to *J2199.5 (MacDonald) Fools (usually animals) invite all comers to join them in abode until house ruptures.* The most well-known variant among U.S. schoolchildren is the Ukrainian tale of the mitten in which all animals squeeze until it breaks. This eggshell boat story also bears similarities to the Siberian tale "Tiny Mouse Goes Traveling," in which a mouse paddles downriver in a nutshell and eats until he bursts. This tale is found in *Look Back and See: Twenty Lively Tales for Gentle Tellers* by Margaret Read Macdonald (New York: H. W. Wilson, 1991), 130–136. A Saudi version is "Passengers of the Eggshell," in *Folktales from Saudi Arabia* by Lamya' Muhammad Salih Ba-ashin (Jiddah: Lamia Baeshen, 2002), 15–18.

THE CAT COUNTRY

This is a variant of *Motif Q.2.1 Kind and unkind girls.* And *Type 480 The Spinning-Woman by the Spring. The Kind and Unkind Girls.* . It has similarities with the Italian tale *Motif Q2.1.1CA (MacDonald) The House of Cats.* The motif of the burp and the tattling cat are intriguing. Because she burps when she bends over, this is probably another rude noise in the original. There is a Saudi version titled "The Matron of Cats," in *Folktales from Saudi Arabia* by Lamya' Muhammad Salih Ba-ashin (Jiddah: Lamia Baeshen, 2002), 90–93.

THE LOST CITY OF UBAR

This story includes a variant of *Motif B210.2.3 (MacDonald) Skull to man: "Talking brought me here." Man claims skull talks. Skull is silent. Man is killed. Man's skull: "Talking brought me here."* There are several African and African American variants of this. A version from Burma tells of a servant told by a beheaded head to go fetch the king. When they return, the head is silent. The servant is beheaded. In the version we give here, the man is imprisoned, rather than beheaded, probably an alteration from the original. Some scholars believe that Shisr (Wubar) might be the site of the lost city of Ubar, though others question that as a possibility. Stories from Oman on pages 47 and 49 are related by a present-day sheik of Shisr, Mahbrook Massan. The Saudi variant is retold from Nadia Taibah and from "The City under the Sands," in *Kuwait and Her Neighbors* by H. R. P. Dickson (London: Routledge, 1956), 498–501. Dickson heard this on April 2, 1943, when Muhammad Ibn Malimm ibn Dráhim al Murri came from Saudi Arabia to visit Dickson in Kuwait.

AZIZ, SON OF HIS MATERNAL UNCLE

This tale is retold and modified slightly from "Aziz Son of His Maternal-Uncle," in *Tales Arab Women Tell* by Hasan M. El-Shamy (Bloomington: Indiana University Press, 1999), 349–355. It was collected by Hasan El-Shamy from Ayasha'Omm H. in the summer of 1986. The narrator was a 70-year-old grandmother who did not read or write. Abu-Zaid, the Hilalite, is a stock character whose epic is popular in the Middle East and in some areas of sub-Saharan Africa. El-Shamy cites versions of this story from Bahrain, Doha, and Qatar. A tale attributed to the Lord Buddha tells of a woman grieving for her lost son who is sent to find a mustard seed from a house that has not known sorrow. *El-Shamy Type 857 Nephew Wins a Bride for his Maternal-uncle: Abu-Zaid Gets Alya; Type844A Search for Household not Touched by Grief.*

> *Motifs: H506.9.1 Test of resourcefulness: making coffee (tea) without water; K514 Disguise as girl to avoid execution; K1817.3 Disguise as harper (minstrel); K137.1.1.2 Lover's foster brother (friend) steals bride from wedding with unwelcome suitor; H1394 Quest for person who has not known sorrow.*

THE SPRINGS OF BAHRAIN

This story is developed from information at http://www.everyculture.com/wc/Afghanistan-to -Bosnia-Herzegovina/Bahrainis.html#ixzz3FCrUh1KA

You can see photos of these children playing in the springs of Bahrain at http://www.folk culturebh.org/en/index.php?issue=14&page=showarticle&id=18.

> *Motif A941 Origin of springs.*

ANSWERING THE SCHOLAR

A version of this tale appears in *Tales of Juha: Classic Arab Folk Humor*, edited by Salma Khadra Jayyusi (Northampton, MA: Interlink, 2007), 85.

> *Motif H881 Riddles with "none" as answer.*

JOUHA SINGS FROM THE MINARET

El-Shamy cites a Turkish story for this. Another version appears in *Tales of Juha: Classic Arab Folk Humor*, edited by Salma Khadra Jayyusi (Northampton, MA: Interlink, 2007), 89.

> *Motif J2237 The bathroom in the minaret. Fool can sing in the bathroom but cannot be heard from the minaret.*

COUNTING THE DAYS OF RAMADAN

A version of this tale appears in *Tales of Juha: Classic Arab Folk Humor*, edited by Salma Khadra Jayyusi (Northampton, MA: Interlink, 2007), 87.

Motif H1118 Task: counting.

CHOICES

This tale is retold from "Son, Husband or Brother?" in *Tales Arab Women Tell* by Hasan M. El-Shamy (Bloomington: Indiana University Press, 1999), 316–317. It was collected in 1982. The informant was a 22-year-old university student from Yemen. She had read the story some months earlier in *Al-Arabi*, a magazine published in Kuwait. Ms. A. R al-Hamadan, a Kuwaiti folklorist, explained that the final phrase from this story is used as a dirge at the death of a brother in Kuwaiti funerals. The tyrant mentioned is al-Hajjaj ibn Yusuf (d. 714), a ruthless ruler of the Omayyad regime.

Type 985 Brother Chosen Rather than Husband or Son.

Motif P253.3 Brother chosen rather than husband or son. Only one can be saved; he alone is irreplaceable.

THE HELPFUL DOG

This tale is retold from "The Pot of Meat," in *Tales Arab Women Tell* by Hasan M. El-Shamy (Bloomington: Indiana University Press, 1999), 103–106. The story was told in August 1970 by Ruqayyah B., a 59-year-old former slave of African heritage living in Kuwait. Hasan M. El-Shamy cites one other Kuwaiti version of this tale.

Type 545 F The Monkey (Dog, Fox, Jackal, etc.) Tests the Fidelity (Gratitude) of its Master.

Motifs: B182.1.0.2 Magic dog transformed person; H1556.1.2 Monkey (fox, jackal, dog, etc.) feigns death (illness) to test master's gratitude; D422.2.1 Transformation: dead dog to money (jewels).

THE BLACK PEARL AND THE WHITE PEARL

This tale is retold from "The Black Pearl and White Pearl," in *The Arab of the Desert: A Glimpse into Badawin Life in Kuwait and Sau'di Arabia* by H. R. P. Dickson (London: George Allen & Unwin, 1949), 492–496. After discussing the pearl-fishing industry, he writes, "The following story is told by mothers to their children in Kuwait." He follows this with a chapter about slavery in Kuwait at that time.

Motif H933 Princess assigns tasks.

KILL THE MAN WHO KILLED THE DOG

This tale is retold from "Kill the Man Who Slew the Dog," in *The Arab of the Desert: A Glimpse into Badawin Life in Kuwait and Sau'di Arabia* by H. R. P. Dickson (London: George Allen & Unwin, 1949), 517–522. Dickson heard the story twice, once from K. B. Mulla Sáleh, wazir to four consecutive rulers of Kuwait, and once from Othmán ibn Humaid al 'Utaibi, a leader among the 'Utaiba tribe.

NESÓP AND THE SNAKE

This tale is told widely around the world. MacDonald and Sturm cite sources from Mexico, Tibet, and Italy and African American sources. Stith Thompson cites sources from Italy, Germany, Spain, India, China, Indonesia, and Africa as well as Jewish and African American sources and Aesop. This folktale is from Kuwait. It was told to H. R. Dickson while camped at Araifjan, on April 1, 1953, by Amsha, the wife of Salim al Muzaiyin. It is retold from *Arab of the Desert: A Glimpse into Badawin Life in Kuwait and Sau'di Arabia* by H. R. P. Dickson (London: George Allen & Unwin, 1949), 36–327.

Motif J1172.3 Ungrateful animal returned to captivity. A man rescues a serpent (bear) who in return seeks to kill his rescuer. Fox as judge advises the man to put the serpent back into captivity. Type 155.The Ungrateful Serpent Returned to Captivity.

THE *HATTÁB* (WOODCUTTER) AND THE *KHAZNAH* (TREASURE)

This is based on a story told to H. R. Dickson by Háji 'Abdullah al Fathil in camp on January 7, 1935. It is retold from *Arab of the Desert: A Glimpse into Badawin Life in Kuwait and Sau'di Arabia* by H. R. P. Dickson (London: George Allen & Unwin, 1949), 315–318. The first episode is from a much longer tale. It is similar to a Thai folktale: "If It Belongs to Us, It Will Come to Us," in *Thai Tales: Folktales of Thailand* by Supaporn Vathanaprida (Englewood, CO: Libraries Unlimited, 1994), 72–74. In the Thai tale, an old man refuses a pot of gold found in a field until robbers dig it up and dump it on his doorstep. The best-known version is retold by Chaucer in "The Pardoner's Tale." MacDonald cites sources from Liberia, the Congo (Luban), and Nigeria. MacDonald and Sturm cite a Chinese variant. Stith Thompson gives variants from Turkey, India, China, Korea, Italy, and others.

Type 763 Two (three) men find a treasure. One of them secretly puts poison in the other's wine (food) but the other kills him, then drinks and dies.

Motifs: N182.1 Man dreams gold falls on head, refuses discovered pot of gold in garden; J2136.5 Careless thief caught; W151.8 Thieves quarrel over booty; N659.2 Poison cakes intended for man by his wife eaten by thieves: booty left to man; K1685 The treasure finders who murder one another.

ABU NAWAS, THE TRICKSTER

This story was collected by JonLee Joseph from Mahbrook Massan in his desert camp on the edge of the Empty Quarter on the evening of September 12, 2010. Mahbrook is a leader in the Shisr community and maintains this camp for visitors in the desert some miles from Shisr. Shisr is the site of archeological remains believed by some to be the lost city of Ubar, which has been much searched for by archeologists over the years. Margaret Read MacDonald heard Mahbrook tell this same story on a visit to his camp in October of 2009.

Motif K362.10 Give him what he wants.

A DJINN STORY

This tale was told to Kiera Anderson and JonLee Joseph in Arabic by Mahbrook Massan on November 28, 2012, in the Empty Quarter, close to Wubar, in Oman. It was translated into English by Kiera Anderson

Motif D1272.1 Magic Line.

JOUHA LOSES HIS DONKEY

This story was shared by Hared Al-Sharji. He heard the story from his grandmother, who lives in the Dhofar Mountains. It was collected by JonLee Joseph. It is retold from *SCT Magazine*, Salalah College of Technology, English Language Center, Salalah, Oman (April 2013), 8. This tale is also told about the Turkish Nasr-din-Hodja.

Motif J2561 Fool thanks God he was not sitting on the ass when it was stolen.

WHO SHOULD RIDE THE DONKEY?

This story was told by the mother of Mohammed Marhoon. Mohammed was a student at the Salalah College of Technology. It was collected by JonLee Joseph. It is retold from *SCT Magazine*, Salalah College of Technology, English Language Center, Salalah, Oman (April 2013), 8. The tale is found throughout Europe and is also told of the Turkish Nasr-din-Hodja.

Motif J1041.2 Miller, his son, and the ass: trying to please everyone.

WHEN JOUHA'S DONKEY PASSES GAS

This tale was told by the father of Reem, a student at Salalah College of Technology. It was collected by JonLee Joseph. It is retold from *SCT Magazine*, Salalah College of Technology, Salalah, Oman (April 2013), 8. For a similar tale, see this Argentinian tale: "When Ingele Believed He Was Dead," in *Pachamama* by Paula Martín (Santa Barbara, CA: Libraries Unlimited, 2014), 82–86.

Type 1240 Man Sitting on Branch of Tree Cuts it off.

Motifs: J2311.1 Numskull told that he will die when his horse breaks wind (or donkey brays) three times. When this happens, he lies down for dead; J2133.4 Numskull cuts off branch on which he is sitting.

THE DJINN OUTSIDE THE WINDOW

This tale was related by Shaika, a student at Salalah College of Technology, and collected by JonLee Joseph. It is retold from *SCT Magazine*, Salalah College of Technology, Salalah, Oman (April 2013), 6.

Motif V229.5 Saint banishes demons [fairies, djinns, etc.].

THE SAD STORY OF THE MOTHER CAMEL

This tale was written down by Said Al-Mahri, a student at Salalah College of Technology. This is told as a true story, not a folktale. It was collected by JonLee Joseph. It was retold from *SCT Magazine*, Salalah College of Technology, Salalah, Oman (April 2013), 15. *Motif B214.4 Weeping animal.*

THE CAMEL FROM THE ROCK

This tale is retold from several sources: "The Miracle of the Camel" by Lady Peter Crowe, *Saudi Aramco World* (September/October 1965), 21; Koran 7:73–78; http://en.wikipedia.org/wiki/Mada%27in_Saleh; http://en.wikipedia.org/wiki/Saleh; http://www.islamicbulletin.org/newsletters/issue_5/salih.aspx; and http://www.sacred-texts.com/isl/bkt/bkt00.htm. This is similar to the biblical tale of Sodom and Gomorrah, in which the cities were destroyed by God because of the evil of their people.

   Q556.0.2 Curse of destruction on city.

THE REMARKABLE CAMEL

Information taken from Daniel da Cruz and Paul Lunde, "The Camel in Retrospect," *Saudi Aramco World* (March/April 1981): 42–48

WHY LOVE IS BLIND

This tale was told by Abdulrahman, a student at Salalah College of Technology, and collected by JonLee Joseph. It is retold from *SCT Magazine*, Salalah College of Technology, Salalah, Oman (April 2013), 9.

THE THRIFTY ANT

This tale was retold by Sufa, a student at Salalah College of Technology, and collected by JonLee Joseph. It is retold from *SCT Magazine*, Salalah College of Technology, Salalah, Oman (April 2013), 10.

   Motif J 191.1 Solomon as wise man.

THE FAKE BRIDE

Stith Thompson includes a variant of this tale from India. Our text is inspired by "The Genie Bride," in *My Grandmother's Stories: Folktales from Dhofar* by Khadija bint Alawi Al-Dhahab (Washington, D.C.: Sultan Qaboos Cultural Center, 2012), 63–65.

   E363.1.1 Ghost substitutes for bride on her wedding journey.

STRANGERS ON THE ROAD

This tale is retold from "Jokes from Muscat and Oman," in *From Town to Tribe* by C. G. Campbell (London: Ernest Benn, 1952), 201–102. It was told by a man of the Hurth tribe of Oman about the Hinawi and Ghafiri tribes.

A JINN BUILDS A ROAD

This tale is retold from "A Joke from Muscat Town," in *From Town to Tribe* by C. G. Campbell (London: Ernest Benn, 1952), 203–204.

In similar European stories, the man usually outsmarts the Devil. The Arabic jinn are a bit more difficult to deal with.

Motifs: F499.4 Jinns; G303.9.1.7 Devil builds a road is related to this tale.

TRICKING THE *SAHAR*

Note that this is a contemporary tale, as the lady is carrying a flashlight and chocolates imported from England. It is retold from "An Account of the Living Creatures," in *Town to Tribe* by C. G. Campbell (London: Ernest Benn, 1952), 101–103.

This is similar to *Motif K1715.7 Demon terrorized by small creatures bluff.*

THE BIGGEST LIE

This tale is retold from "Also from Muscat Town," in *Town to Tribe* by C. G. Campbell (London: Ernest Benn, 1952), 204–205.

Type 1920A The first tells of a giant cabbage. The second of a giant kettle to cook it in.

Motifs: X1150.1 The great catch of fish; X1423.1 Lie: the great cabbage. Matched by the tale of great pot to put cabbage in.

THE HELPFUL FISH

This story is found as "Fsaijrah," in *Tales Arab Women Tell* by Hasan M. El-Shamy (Bloomington: Indiana University Press, 1999), 278–279. The folklorist Hasan El-Shamy was given this story in June 1973 in a written version from a contributor who gave her name only as "A Qatari Princess." The royal family in Qatar is numerous, and there are many princesses. El-Shamy cites 48 versions from Arabic tellers, including 5 others from Qatar. A second version of this story appears in *The Donkey Lady and Other Tales of the Arabian Gulf*, edited by Patty Paine, Jesse Ulmer, and Michael Hersud. Collected and translated by Khamam Al Ghanem and Dr. Sara Al-Mohannadi (Berkshire, U.K.: Berkshire Academic Press, Limited, 2013), 17–36. For a picture book version, see *Hamda and Fisaikra* by Dr. Kaltham al Ghanem, with illustrations by May al Mannai (Doha, Qatar: Bloomsbury Qatar Foundation, 2011).

Type 510 Cinderella.

Motifs: B375.1 Fish returned to water: grateful; B470.1 Small fish as helper.

WEALTH, SUCCESS, AND LOVE

A version of this tale appears in *The Donkey Lady and Other Tales of the Arabian Gulf*, edited by Patty Paine, Jesse Ulmer, and Michael Hersud. Collected and translated by Maryam Mubarek Al Muhaiza and Dr. Sara Al-Mohannadi (Berkshire, U.K.: Berkshire Academic Press, Limited, 2013), 209–213.

Motifs: H659.7 Riddle: what is greatest?; H648 Riddle: what is best? Hasan M. El-Shamy's *Folk Traditions of the Arab World* (Bloomington: Indiana University Press, 1995) cites versions of *H630ff Riddles of the superlative* from Egypt, Iraq, Morocco Palestine, Saudi Arabia, Syria, and Yemen

ORIGIN OF THE DHOW'S LATEEN SAIL

See this article for more on the origin of the lateen sail: http://en.wikipedia.org/wiki/Lateen. A version of this tale may be found in *The Donkey Lady and Other Tales of the Arabian Gulf*, edited by Patty Paine, Jesse Ulmer, and Michael Hersud. Collected and translated by Mariam Mohammed Al-Kuwari and Dr. Sara Al-Mohannadi (Berkshire, U.K.: Berkshire Academic Press, Limited, 2013), 73–91.

WHY THE HEN CANNOT FLY

This tale is retold from *Folklore and Folklife in the United Arab Emirates* by Sayyid H. Hurreíz (London, Routledge Curzon, 2002).

Motif A2331 Animal characteristics: punishment for impiety.

THE SHAIKH'S SHEEP

A version of this tale appears in *Folklore and Folklife in the United Arab Emirates* by Sayyid H. Hurreíz (London: Routledge Curzon, 2002).

Motifs: H588 Enigmatic counsels of a father; K2213.4 Betrayal of husband's secret by wife.

THE FISHERMAN'S DAUGHTER

This is a variant of *Type 510 Cinderella*. An Arabian version is found in "The Fisherman's Daughter," in *Folklore and Folklife in the United Arab Emirates* by Sayyid H. Hurreiz (London: Routledge Curzon, 2003), 74–75. The fish in that story is called *Al bideha*.

THE QUEEN OF SHEBA VISITS SOLOMON

The Queen of Sheba is believed to be the queen Bilquis of Saba in present-day Yemen. You can read more details in the Old Testament, First Book of Kings, chapter 10, and in the Koran, sura 27.

Motifs: H540.2.1 Queen of Sheba propounds riddle to Solomon; H561.3.1 King Solomon as master riddle-solver.

QUEEN BILQUIS VISITS KING SUYLEIMAN

Stith Thompson gives Greek and Japanese variants of this tale. This story is found in the Old Testament, First Book of Kings, chapter 10, and in the Koran, sura 27. An expanded retelling is "Queen Balqis and King Sulayman," in *Fabled Cities, Princes & Jinn from Arab Myths and Legends* by Khairat Al-Saleh (New York: Schocken, 1985) 50–57.

Motifs: H540.2.1 Queen of Sheba propounds riddle to Solomon; H561.3.1 King Solomon as master riddle-solver; H506.4 Test of resourcefulness: putting thread through coils of snail shell. Thread tied to ant who pulls it through.

THE MIGHTY DIKE OF MA-RIB

One source for this tale is "Ma-rib": http://www.britannica.com/EBchecked/topic/364999/ Marib. A good retelling appears in "The Queen Priestess and the Dyke of Ma'rib," in *Fabled Cities, Princes & Jinn: Arab Myths and Legends* by Kairat Al-Saleh (New York: Shocken Books, 1985), 57–59. It is also found in "The Great and Terrible Wilderness" by Immanuel Velicovsky: http://www.varchive.org/ce/baalbek/desert.htm. And the incident is mentioned in the Koran, sura 34.

Motif V17.5 Sacrifice to get knowledge.

THE YEAR OF THE WHITE ELEPHANT

Versions of this tale can be found in the following: "The Year of the Elephant," in *Fabled Cities, Princes & Jinn from Arab Myths and Legends* by Kairat Al-Saleh (New York: Schocken, 1985), 64–66; "Al-qalis," in *From the Land of Sheba: Yemeni Folk Tales* by Carolyn Han. Translated by Kamal Ali al-Hegri (Northampton, MA: Interlink, 2005), 52–55; the Koran, sura 105; and http:// answering-islam.org/Books/Al-Kalbi/qalis.htm. For historical background on Abraha, see the *Wikipedia* link http://en.wikipedia.org/wiki/Abraha. An inscription on the dam at Ma'rib tells that Abraha repaired the dam.

THE MANLY MAIDEN

Variants of this tale appear in many collections of *The Arabian Nights*. The story is a variant of *Type 881A The Abandoned Bride Disguised as a Man*. It includes *Motifs: K521.4.1.1 Girl escapes in male disguise; K1236 Disguise as man to escape importunate lover; K1837.8 Woman in man's disguise made king; K1837 Disguise of woman in man's clothing; K1322 Girl masked as man wins princesses love; H21 Recognition through picture. Picture is publicly displayed and brings about recognition of lost person.* One version of this tale is found in *The Land of Sheba* by S. D. Goitein (New York: Schocken Books, 1947), 67–91.

PROVERBS FROM THE UNITED ARAB EMIRATES

Proverbs are taken from: Fuad Rayess, "The Cream of Wisdom," *Saudi Aramco World* (January/February 1969), 22–25 and from *Folklife in the United Arab Emirates* by Sayyid H. Hurreiz (London: Routledge Curzon), 84–85.

HUNAIN'S SLIPPERS

This proverb tale is retold from "The Cream of Wisdom" by Fuad Rayess, *Saudi Aramco World* (January/February 1969), 22–25.

A CRAB WHO DROWNED A CAMEL

This is an Omani folktale, retold from "The Crab That Drowned a Camel," in *From Town and Tribe* by C. G. Campbell (London: Benn, 1952), 99.

RIDDLES

Sources of the riddles include the following: *Arab Folklore: A Handbook* by Dwight Fletcher Reynolds (Westwood, CT: Greenwood Press, 2007), 118–119; and *Folklore and Folklife in the United Arab Emirates* by Sayyid H. Hurreiz (London: Routledge Curzon), 84–85.

ARABIC WORDS

This information was taken from Alan Pimm-Smith, "From Ar'abic to Eng'lish," *Saudi Aramco World* (March/April 2007), 36–38.

MORE FOLKTALES FROM THE ARABIAN PENINSULA

Alawi Al-Dhahab, Khadija bint. *My Grandmother's Stories: Folk Tales from Dhofar.* Illustrated by Fatima bint Alawi Muqaybil. Washington, D.C.: Sultan Qaboos Cultural Center. www.sqcc.org.

Al-Ghanim, Kaltham. *Hamda and Fisaikra.* Illustrated by May al-Mannai. Doha, Qatar: Bloomsbury Qatar Foundation, 2011. (Available in both English and Arabic editions.)

Al-Saleh, Khairat. *Fabled Cities, Princes & Jinn from Arab Myths and Legends.* New York: Schocken, 1985. Beautifully retold, with illustrations by Rashad N. Salim.

Busnaq, Inea. *Arab Folktales.* New York: Pantheon, 1986. (This adult collection includes tales from North Africa, Iraq, Syria, and Palestine. There are only a few from the Arabian Peninsula.)

Conover, Sarah, and Freda Crane. *Ayat Jamilah: Beautiful Signs: A Treasury of Islamic Wisdom for Children and Parents.* Cheney, WA: Eastern Washington University, 2010.

Demi. *Muhammad.* New York: Margaret K. McElderry Books, 2002.

Han, Carolyn. *From the Land of Sheba: Yemeni Folk Tales.* Translated by Kamal Ali al-Hegri. Northampton, MA: Interlink, 2005.

Jayyusi, Salma Khadra, ed. *Tales of Juha: Classic Arab Folk Humor.* Northampton, MA: Interlink, 2007.

Johnson-Davies, Denys. *Goha the Wise Fool.* Illustrated by Hag Hamdy Mohamed Fattou and Hany El Saed Ahmed. New York: Philomel, 2005. Compare these Egyptian tales with our Jouha tales. These are illustrated by tent makers from Cairo.

MacDonald, Margaret Read, and Nadia Jameel Taibah. *How Many Donkeys?: An Arabic Counting Tale.* Illustrated by Carol Liddiment. Chicago: Albert Whitman, 2009.

Paine, Patty, Jesse Ulmer, and Michael Hersud. *The Donkey Lady and Other Tales of the Arabian Gulf.* Collected and translated by Khamam Al Ghanem and Dr. Sara Al-Mohannadi. Berkshire, U.K.: Berkshire Academic Press, Limited, 2013, 17–36.

Todino-Gonguet, Grace. *Halimah and the Snake and Other Omani Folk Tales.* Illustrated by Susan Keeble. London: Stacey International, 2008.

BIBLIOGRAPHY

Aarne, Antti, and Stith Thompson. *The Types of the Folktale*. Helsinki: Suomalainen Tiedeakatemia, 1973.

Al-Dhahab, Khadija bint Alawi. *My Grandmother's Stories: Folktales from Dhofar*. Washington, D.C.: Sultan Qaboos Cultural Center, 2012, 63–65.

Al-Saleh, Khairat. *Fabled Cities, Princes & Jinn from Arab Myths and Legends*. New York: Schocken, 1985.

Ba-ashin, Lamya Muhammad Salih. *Folktales from Saudi Arabia*. Jiddah: Lamia Baeshen, 2002.

Campbell, C. G. *From Town and Tribe*. London: Benn, 1952.

Crowe, Lady Peter. "The Miracle of the Camel," *Saudi Aramco World*, September/October 1965, 21.

Cruz, Daniel da, and Paul Lunde. "The Camel in Retrospect," *Saudi Aramco World*, March/April 1981, 42–48.

Dickson, H. R. P. *The Arab of the Desert: A Glimpse into Badawin Life in Kuwait and Sau'di Arabia*. London: George Allen & Unwin, 1949.

Dickson, H. R. P. *Kuwait and Her Neighbors*. London: George Allen & Unwin, 1956.

El-Shamy, Hasan M. *Folk Traditions of the Arab World: A Guide to Motif Classification*. Bloomington: Indiana University Press, 1995.

El-Shamy, Hasan M. *Tales Arab Women Tell*. Bloomington: Indiana University Press, 1999.

Goitein, S. D. *From the Land of Sheba*. New York: Schocken Books, 1973.

Han, Carolyn. *From the Land of Sheba: Yemeni Folk Tales*. Translated by Kamal Ali al-Hegri. Northampton, MA: Interlink, 2005.

The Holy Koran: An Interpretive Translation from Classical Arabic into Contemporary English. Phoenix, AZ: Acacia Publishing, 2008.

Hurreíz, Sayyid H. *Folklore and Folklife in the United Arab Emirates*. London: Routledge Curzon, 2002.

The Illuminated Bible: Text of the Authorized King James Version. Chicago: Columbia Educational Books, Inc., 1941

Jayyusi, Salma Khadra, ed. *Tales of Juha: Classic Arab Folk Humor*. Northampton, MA: Interlink, 2007

Lunde, Paul. "Aesop of the Arabs," *Saudi Aramco World*, March/April 1974, 2–3.

MacDonald, Margaret Read. *The Storyteller's Sourcebook: A Subject, Title, and Motif Index to Folklore Collections for Children*. 1st ed. Detroit: Gale Research, 1982.

MacDonald, Margaret Read, and Brian W. Sturm. *The Storyteller's Sourcebook: A Subject, Title, and Motif Index to Folklore Collections for Children: 1983–1999*. Detroit: Gale Research, 2000.

Paine, Patty, Jesse Ulmer, and Michael Hersud, eds. *The Donkey Lady and Other Tales of the Arabian Gulf*. Collected and translated by Khamam Al Ghanem and Dr. Sara Al-Mohannadi. Berkshire, U.K.: Berkshire Academic Press, Limited, 2013, 17–36.

Pimm-Smith, Alan. "From Ar'abic to Eng'lish," *Saudi Aramco World*, March/April 2007, 36–38.

Rayess, Faud. "The Cream of Wisdom," *Saudi Aramco World*, January/February 1969, 22–25.

Reynolds, Dwight Fletcher. *Arab Folklore: A Handbook*. Westport, CT: Greenwood Press, 2007.

SCT Magazine. Salalah College of Technology, English Language Center, Salalah, Oman (April 2013).

Thompson, Stith. *Motif-Index of Folk-Literature*. Bloomington: Indiana University Press, 1966.

Tracy, William. "A Talk with Violet Dickson," *Saudi Aramco World*. November/December 1972, 13–19.

INDEX

Fox, as judge 45–46; gives lion bigger share, 3
"The Fox, the Wolf, and the Lion," 3
Frankincense, x, xix
Fsaijrah goes to party, 63

Genie substitutes daughter for bride, 58
Ghafiri tribe, 59
Ghoul threatens, 16–17
Girl in guise of man weds princess, 79
Girl, poor marries prince, 38–39
Gold mouse droppings, 23
Goldfinch tells wife tales to warn, 75
Grief, house without, 30
Gulf War, xiii

Hadith xx, 81
Hadramat, xix
Hajj, xi, xii, xvi, xvii
Haram, xvii
"The Hattáb (Woodcutter) and the
    Khaznah (Treasure), 46
Heart, most valuable and least, xix
"The Helpful Dog," 38–39
"The Helpful Fish," 63
Hen refuses to say "Insha'allah," 67
Herodotus, x
Hijaz, xvi
Hinawi tribe, 59
Hoopoe bird tells of Saba, 72
"Hunan's Slippers," 82
Hurth tribe, 59

Ibrahim, Prophet, xvii
Isa, Prophet (Jesus), xvii
Islam, xii; required for citizenship, xi
Ismael, xvii

Jabal an Nabi Shu-ayb, xix
Jaed, girl wearing, 16
Jebel, color inset
Jeddah, xi
Jewelry left for Abu Nawas, 47
Jinn brings throne, 72
"The Jinn Builds a Road," 60
Joseph, JonLee, 47, 49, 114, color inset
Jouha, 7, 33–36, 51

"Jouha and His Donkeys," 7
"Jouha Loses His Donkey," 50
Judge dances, 8–9
Judgement, kill man who killed dog,
    43–44; shepherd to till land, farmer to guard
    sheep, 20

Ka'ba, xi, xii, xvi, xvii, attacked, 74
Khoja Nasruddin al-Rumi, 33
"Kill the Man Who Killed the Dog," 43–44
"The King, the Prince, and the Naughty
    Sheep," 20
Knowledge chosen over childbearing, 73
Koran, xvii, 54, 72, 81
Kuwait, xiii, 27, 33–46
Kuwait children's program, color inset
Kuwait city photos, xii
Kuwaiti scenes, b & w inset
Kuwaiti tenting, xiv, xv, color inset
Kuwaiti villa, color inset

Language of animals understood by
    Suleiman, 20
Lateen sail, origin, 65
Leopard has water inside body, 47
Lie, biggest, 62
Line, drawn, crossed, 49
Lion eats wolf, fox learns to divide, 3
Liwa oasis, xvii
"The Lost City of Ubar," 27–28
Louse complains that ant hit, 4
Love has eye poked out by Madness, 56
Love most important, 64
"Luqman the Wise," xix–xx

MacDonald, Margaret Read, 113; photo,
    color inset
Madness pokes out eye of Love, 56
"Makki and Khakki," 23
Maktoum family, xvii
Man disguised as woman, 30
"The Manly Maid," 75–80
"The Mighty Dyke of Ma-rib," 73
Ma-rib dyke, 73
Massan, Mahbrook, x, 47, 49
Mecca, xi, xii, xvi, 21; attacked, 74

About the Authors

Margaret Read MacDonald, a folklore Ph.D. and former children's librarian, has worked with storytellers from Argentina, Brazil, Cuba, Indonesia, Laos, Malaysia, Singapore, and Thailand to create folktale collections for the Libraries Unlimited World Folktales series. While working on this collection from the Arabian Peninsula, she was fortunate to make several visits to the area, telling stories and traveling in Abu-Dhabi, Bahrain, Dubai, Kuwait, Oman, Qatar, and Saudi Arabia. Her Arabic counting book *How Many Donkeys?*, coauthored with Nadia Jameel Taibah, won the 2010 Sharjah International Book Fair Award for Best English Language Children's Book dealing with an Arabic topic.

Nadia Jameel Taibah is an assistant professor at King Abdul-Aziz University in Jeddah, Saudi Arabia. She received her doctorate in special education, learning disabilities, from the University of Washington. Her interests in helping children to be literate and include reading stories as part of their lives led her to become specialized in reading and specifically diagnosing children with reading disabilities. She is involved in many national projects to develop and standardize assessment tools for reading and reading-related skills. She was raised hearing some of these stories from her family, especially her mother, Zain, and aunt Salha.

Contributor **JonLee Joseph** taught English at Salalah College of Technology in Salalah, Oman, for five years. While there, JonLee spent time visiting the rural homes of her students and their families. She even bought two camels of her own, which she could visit and care for. She encouraged her students to share stories they had heard from their families. On overnight trips to a desert camp on the edge of the Rub Al-Khali, she collected stories from Mahbrook Massan, a sheik of Shifr.

RECENT TITLES IN THE WORLD FOLKLORE SERIES

Additional titles in this series can be found at www.abc-clio.com